Headless Chickens, Laidback Bears

If you want to know how...

Resolving Conflict

Establish trusting and productive relationships in the work place

2-4-6-8, How do you Communicate?

How to make your point in just a minute

Becoming a Director

Learn the basics and become an effective director

Making Management Simple

A practical handbook for meeting management challenges

howtobooks

for full details, please send for a free copy of the latest catalogue to:
How To Books Ltd, 3 Newtec Place,
Magdalen Road, Oxford OX4 1RE. United Kingdom

Headless Chickens, Laidback Bears

Scientific techniques to create more time and revolutionise your life and work

Gordon Wainwright

howtobooks

Published by
How To Books Ltd, 3 Newtec Place,
Magdalen Road, Oxford OX4 1RE. United Kingdom
Tel: (01865) 793806. Fax: (01865) 248780
Email: info@howtobooks.co.uk
http://www.howtobooks.co.uk

First edition 2004

British Library Cataloguing in Publication Data
A catalogue record for this book is available from the British Library

Produced for How To Books by Deer Park Productions, Tavistock
Cover design by Baseline Arts Ltd, Oxford
Typeset by Baseline Arts Ltd, Oxford
Printed and bound by Bell & Bain Ltd, Glasgow

Contents

INTRODUCTION

Time Creation, as it is defined in this book, is another name for the science of chronemics, the study of how we use our time and of how we may use it more effectively. But it is more than this. It is a set of techniques for doing things in time-saving ways.

> *Time Creation will, literally, change your life if you put it into practice. It will change it for the better. Improve your use of time and you will cease to be one of life's headless chickens who dash round looking busy but achieving little, and become one of its laidback bears who really get things done and enjoy life at the same time.*

It is the purpose of this book to show you how.

These techniques are needed, now more than ever, because the world is going through a period of rapid change. If anything, the rate of change is increasing exponentially – that is to say, changes are affecting the way we live and work faster and faster each year.

So, the pace of life is increasing partly as a result of the rate of change and partly because that's the way a high-technology, sophisticated society like ours functions. Developments in electronics, for instance, have enabled information to be produced in quantities and at speeds that seemed inconceivable not much more than a decade ago. The development of high-speed transport, particularly by rail and by air, has meant that, technology permitting, you can be on the other side of the globe in less than a day or across a country in a very few hours.

If we are to keep up with this rate of change and this pace of life, we need to acquire new techniques and skills that our parents and grandparents had no need for. Greater speed of activity is being thrust upon us whether we like it or not and we have two choices. We can ignore it and turn our backs on the world and go down bravely, or we can develop the techniques which will enable us to cope. Time Creation is for those who make the second choice.

Not that the objective is to make you even more like a headless chicken dashing hither and thither with no real sense of purpose, or a rat in a rat race which is being turned ever faster. It is, rather, to enable you to speed up those activities that can sensibly be speeded up and to identify ways of saving time in carrying out those that cannot. The objective is that, in doing this, you will become one of life's laidback bears and be able to cope. In addition, you will be able to create some discretionary time – that is, time which you can spend in whatever way takes your fancy. You may use it to get more work done (especially if you work for yourself), or to think about work-related problems which you don't normally have the time to think about, or to engage in your favourite leisure activity, or just to sit and daydream. The choice is yours. You may even use it to acquire greater mastery of Time Creation techniques.

These techniques are often essentially simple, common-sense ones that can be easily learned. They can be self-taught without difficulty, as you will see as you work your way through this book. Some of them have technical names given them by scientific researchers in chronemics or in some other sub-discipline of the behavioural sciences. Where this happens, they will usually also be given an alternative simpler name which those readers who wisely prefer to avoid all jargon can use. The purpose here is, in other words, to provide you with a very sound, practical guide to time-management techniques which you can use without having to rely upon the support of a tutor or counsellor.

There are, in fact, very few tutors available who could help you. Chronemics is a very young science and is not yet widely known in the UK. Indeed, speed has always been a neglected aspect of education and training. Many teachers still have a deep suspicion of techniques that help people to think faster, read faster, write faster or do anything else faster. They concentrate on teaching you to do these things well. They often give little thought to helping you to do them well and quickly. It is high time that speed was emphasised a good deal more strongly in our educational system than it has been hitherto.

This is not to argue, however, that *everything* should be done faster. We need to remember that sometimes it is better to slow down. One can only do this if one uses Time Creation techniques to create the time for doing so. Just as in driving a car, there are times when speed is appropriate and times when it is not. No one is arguing for speed for speed's sake. It is as ridiculous to suggest, for instance, that you should read quickly all the time as it would be to suggest that you should read slowly all the time.

Given a reasonable (though by no means a fanatical) degree of commitment to applying the techniques, you should notice some benefit from Time Creation almost straight away. Some techniques work sooner than others, but they should all show results after a week or so if they are going to work. This last qualification has to be made because few of the techniques will work equally well for everyone. But even if only some of them work for you, this does not matter too much. Benefit will still be obtained from those which do work and this will help you to cope better with the rate of change and the pace of life. There can be no guarantee in any kind of training that any particular techniques will work equally well for everybody. Try each one out and build on those that work for you.

Most people will find that they can achieve a 25% increase in speed in most activities without any loss in the quality of performance. In some, like reading, a 100% increase is by no means uncommon and the benefits that can result from that kind of improvement can be immeasurable and lifelong. In others, the increase may only be 5% or 10% but even this is worth having. If something takes on average half an hour and there are three such activities a day, a 10% increase in speed (or reduction in time spent on each one) can save almost 55 hours a year. This can be the equivalent of $1\frac{1}{2}$ working weeks, 11 five-hour games of golf, nearly 37 football matches or about 15 books read that otherwise would not have been enjoyed. If this is the kind of benefit which can accrue from a small increase in speed, you can imagine the benefits to be gained from using Time Creation techniques in all your daily activities at work and during leisure time. You may also begin to realise that time creation is designed not to imprison but to liberate.

You can start working on this book in a number of ways. You can read through all of it first before trying to put anything into practice. You can study the chapters in Part 1 (reading Chapter 1 first) and try to practise each technique as soon as you learn it. Or you can read Part 1 and then move to Part 3 and try to use the techniques on those skills where you are most in need of increases in speed. However, unless you have a particular preference in the choice of an approach, you will probably do best to work through the book from the beginning, chapter by chapter.

Before you start, however, it might help if we briefly review what you are likely to encounter in each part of the book. This kind of preview, in fact, should be the result of using the techniques described in Chapter 4 of Part 1 (anticipatory scanning techniques). It is nearly always easier to process information if you have some idea of its general nature in advance.

Part 1, 'Time Creation Techniques', presents the twelve basic techniques. Each chapter introduces a technique and shows you how to use it more effectively.

In Part 2, 'Overcoming Problems in Using Time Creation Techniques', most of the difficulties that you are likely to encounter in mastering the techniques are identified and ways of overcoming them are discussed. You will be able to pay particular attention to those which you have experienced and be able to take effective action to deal with them.

Part 3, 'Applications in Personal Skills', shows how Time Creation techniques can be applied in a variety of essential skills in order to increase speed of performance without experiencing loss of quality or efficiency.

Part one:
Time Creation Techniques

This part of the book explains the various time creation techniques, gives examples of how and where they can be used and suggests exercises for developing skill in using them. As the techniques are learned and practised, they build up into a strategic approach to saving time and making the transition from headless chicken to laidback bear.

Chapter one

ACCURATE FEEDBACK

You have to know how well or badly you are doing. The quicker and more accurately you can find out, the faster and the better you can perform, whatever the task. For this reason, if for no other, accurate feedback is essential in any task or activity.

> *We can define feedback as information coming back to an individual which enables him or her to assess performance and attempt any modifications necessary to improve it. This information may be communicated by others (as when a student receives examination results) or it may result from an individual's own observations (as when, in writing a letter or a report, you read over what you have written and correct any mistakes).*

Some feedback can be unsought (as when you burn your fingers on an iron that you assumed was cool), but we shall be mainly concerned here with feedback that is deliberately sought in order to speed up activities or tasks.

Research has shown that it is a characteristic of skilled performers in many activities that they appear to know what is happening at any stage of a task, that they take pains to check their performance periodically and that they consult others in order to obtain further feedback which may well, since it is a second opinion, be more objective and reliable.

No one really understands how feedback on behaviour works in making improved performance possible, but the fact remains that it does. It seems to be an indispensable part of any learning process. It may be that what is usually referred to as the central processing part of the brain uses information obtained about actions to modify subsequent behaviour in some subtle way so as to permit smoother, problem-free performance and the achievement of a greater degree of skill.

The mechanism by which this kind of information is obtained is usually called a feedback loop and there is a need to provide for such loops in learning models. The flexible performance strategy **PAPA-ROMEO-OSCAR** which we shall encounter later in more detail is an example of such a model. The main feedback loop in that can be illustrated thus:

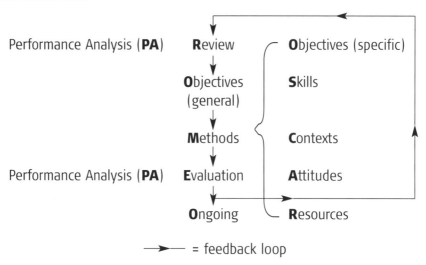

Performance Analysis (**PA**) **R**eview — **O**bjectives (specific)

Objectives (general) **S**kills

Methods **C**ontexts

Performance Analysis (**PA**) **E**valuation **A**ttitudes

Ongoing **R**esources

⟶— = feedback loop

In other words, the information you gain from evaluating your performance after a period of training can help you to decide whether to proceed to the 'Ongoing' stage or to return to the 'Review' stage and repeat the process, making such modifications at each stage as are necessary. This is a broad application of the principle of feedback loops, but it could well be in many activities that there should be a feedback loop between each stage back to the previous one, so that you can make more frequent but smaller adjustments in approach. An example of where this would be desirable would be in applying the P–R–O approach to improving decision-making ability, where feedback might be needed on each decision made.

Research shows that knowledge of results is desirable in any activity, but especially in learning experiences. Where people are kept in the dark about how well or how badly they are doing it becomes extremely difficult for them to make progress. If feedback is denied, as when a teacher fails to mark students' exercises regularly and as soon after the work is done as practicable, bad habits are acquired which then become highly resistant to change, faults persist, individuals lose motivation and performance generally deteriorates.

You do not need to become obsessed about obtaining feedback, however. Just build it in to your approach. A simple method is to select an activity. Tackle it in a reasonably relaxed way. Don't try to do better, but don't try not to. A little effort will not go amiss, but don't get into a situation where the more you try the worse you get. Aim for smooth, confident, flowing action. Recite to yourself what is happening, keep your objectives in mind and let your brain do the rest.

Sometimes feedback can mislead, especially if you make a false connection between cause and effect. For example, if you walk under a ladder and some paint falls on you, faulty feedback might lead you to conclude that it is always unlucky to walk under ladders. A more rational use of feedback would be to conclude that, when walking under ladders, you simply need to keep your wits about you. If someone is painting overhead, then on that occasion it may be sensible to walk round rather than under.

You should also guard against becoming too conditioned by feedback. In his book, *The Mechanism of Mind*, Edward de Bono, the originator of 'lateral thinking', likens the operation of the mind to a jelly. Trickle hot water over a jelly and a pathway is melted out. Trickle more water over it and this water will tend to follow the path created by the first trickle. In other words, feedback can make you react in stereotyped ways if you are not careful to appreciate the unique characteristics that differentiate one situation from another. Because an approach has worked on one occasion does not mean that it is the best one to use on another, so feedback needs to be treated with some caution.

You need to remember that there are two kinds of feedback.

1. Positive feedback, or reward, tells you that things are going well.
2. Negative feedback, or punishment, tells you they are going wrong and that some form of corrective action must be taken.

You can use a combination of both to strengthen desirable behaviour patterns and weaken undesirable ones. For instance, you can reward yourself in some way (it need only be small, a sweet or something else you like) every time you beat a previous best time for an activity or finish before a deadline, and you can punish yourself (by foregoing a favourite TV programme, say) when you fail. It is worth remembering, though, that research evidence suggests quite strongly that rewards are much more effective in developing desirable behaviour patterns than are punishments. As the old quip has it, the best way to knock a chip off a person's shoulder is to pat them on the back.

Not only is positive feedback better than negative feedback, but any kind of feedback is better than none at all. Generally speaking, where feedback is unavailable or removed, performance deteriorates. Where the amount given is increased, performance improves (always bearing in mind the qualifications expressed above).

The best kind of feedback is continuous and immediate, so that you know straight away how well you are doing. It makes faster responses possible, and allows for errors to be made with enough time to be able to remedy them.

Feedback is, in fact, almost a training method on its own. Given clear objectives and a choice of proven methods, the provision of accurate feedback can take you a long way towards your goals.

As far as obtaining feedback is concerned, there is a wide choice of methods and some have already been mentioned, but others can be suggested.

- You can use tests to find out how well you are doing.
- You can make your own observations of what happens.
- You can make sound or video recordings of activities.
- You can obtain the observations and comments of other people.
- You can rely upon a 'gut' feeling about the success or otherwise of a response.
- Perhaps the simplest and most effective way is to keep records in a notebook.

Where you obtain timings and other results, it can help to record them in graph or chart form. A pictorial record of some kind is more useful to most people than a simple tabulation of results. Such a record will help you to monitor your progress sensibly, especially if you consult it regularly.

No method can succeed entirely, no matter how good it is, unless you are prepared to be flexible and to make changes in your behaviour in the light of what the feedback tells you. The attitude you need is one in which you are always actively seeking ways to enable you to make faster responses and so achieve a better performance. Given this, accurate feedback can form the basis of your collection of effective time creation techniques.

If you really are a headless chicken, the sooner you find out the better. Then you can really do something to begin becoming more of a laidback bear.

Chapter two
FLOW RATES

All human activity is based on information processing. Whatever we do, whether it is an automatic activity like breathing or a complex and highly sophisticated activity like solving a philosophical problem, our brains are required to process vast amounts of information.

> *The brain can be looked upon as an information-processing machine. How well it performs this task is affected considerably by the rate at which it receives information. This rate is called here the flow rate.*

Time creation is concerned with identifying and applying ways in which the flow rate can be speeded up. It aims to achieve this without adverse effects upon the quality of performance. Often, in fact, a higher flow rate produces better performance because the brain is being used at a speed which is closer to its true potential. Sometimes the flow rate needs to be slowed down and this is still a concern of time creation. Time creation is concerned with doing things at the optimum speed, bearing in mind the nature of the activity and the context in which it is being carried out. It is not interested in fast living or doing things faster just for the sake of doing them faster. Speed for the sake of speed is one of the factors that produces headless chickens in the first place.

The flow rate can take many forms. It is concerned with both receiving information and producing it. In receiving information, as in reading, it is affected by how quickly the eyes move across the page, how many reading materials are dealt with in a given time, and so on. In producing information, as in taking part in a discussion or meeting, it is affected by how often an individual speaks (or what is often called the contribution rate), how much is said on each occasion (or volume production), and so on.

Flow rate can be increased in a number of ways. Shortage of time may mean things have to be done faster. There may be an increase in the 'information density' (as, for instance, in reading, when one paragraph may contain a lot more information than others). It may also be increased deliberately. It is this last method that we are interested in here.

Before you can try to raise your flow rate, you will need two things. You will need them for every chapter in this book, so you should make sure you have them to hand every time you are working on developing time creation techniques.

You will need a means of timing activities. A stopwatch or a digital watch or clock which has a timer facility will give you the necessary degree of precision. Accurate measurement is necessary because you cannot tell merely from a subjective impression whether you are doing things faster or not. You may think you are doing something faster and then find you have in fact taken longer over it. So a means of making objective measurements of time and speed is essential. You can, of course, use any old clock or watch if you like, but you will sacrifice some accuracy in the process.

You will also need a notebook in which to record your performance. This is necessary so that you can have continuous and accurate feedback, the reasons for which we explained in more detail in Part 1 Chapter 1. Record starting times and finishing times for activities and everything else that you are instructed to record as you work through this book. In this way, you will make faster and better progress in mastering time creation techniques.

Let us now see, then, how the flow rate can be increased. Select an activity, any activity. Getting a meal ready, reading the morning paper, walking from the train to the office, writing a letter, putting your make-up on, or any other activity which you would like to do faster.

1. Set a starting time which will enable you to proceed uninterrupted.

2. Set your stopwatch or timer in motion.

3. Carry out the activity as you would normally do it and record the amount of time it takes you.

4. Choose a way of assessing how well you have performed and record this in the notebook as well.

5. Reading can be checked by a comprehension test. Other activities can be graded by yourself or, better still, by someone else, on a scale of 0 to 10 for quality.

On the second and subsequent occasions, you simply try to increase the flow rate by faster movements. As you do the activity, try to do everything just a little faster than you would normally do things. Don't try to do anything differently at this stage, just faster. Faster movements are a very simple way of raising the flow rate. Be careful not to overdo it. A 5% or 10% increase in speed is the most we are looking for from this technique. Anything more and you might start to make mistakes. We do not want that. We want a higher flow rate without errors.

Concentrate on the chosen activity until it is completed. Don't try to do several things at once. Don't stop. Don't go back if, for instance, you have chosen an activity like reading, to check on parts you have already dealt with. Going back (or regression) is rarely necessary and, since it clearly adds to the time an activity takes, it is better to aim for regression-free progress. On each occasion, at the end of the activity, record the time taken, together with your assessment of the quality of performance. Do this for at least three days before adding on the next time creation technique to your approach.

Remember that being able to do things faster does not mean that you *always* have to do them faster. But it helps when you have to. It also gives better performance when doing them slightly slower than you know you are capable of doing them. This is because once the pressure for faster movement is relaxed slightly you can often enjoy an activity more, knowing that if the time available for it is curtailed without warning you are able to speed up without making errors and still complete the task satisfactorily.

In situations where the flow rate is controlled by others, for instance when watching television, on train journeys, in lectures or on mass-production lines, there is less scope for faster movement, but there is still some. On TV, subtitles can be read quicker, the point or purpose of a play can be perceived quicker, questions on quiz shows can be answered (or attempted) before the participants respond. On train journeys books can be read quicker, snacks taken slightly faster, more letters can be written. In lectures, notes can be made faster and on mass-production lines there is still some scope for faster movement to enable one to be just slightly ahead of the pace of the line so that extra mini-breaks can be taken while the line catches up.

When you proceed to the next time creation technique, it is vital to remember that you do not give all of your attention to that technique and forget about this one. The aim is, rather, to add on the next technique to this one, so that by the time you reach the end of Part 1 Chapter 12 you are practising twelve new techniques. That way, you will get the greatest possible benefit out of time creation and move gradually and certainly from being a headless chicken to becoming a laidback bear for whom speed has a purpose and is used when necessary. Anyone who has watched on TV grizzly bears fishing in a river for salmon knows how quickly bears can move when they have to.

chapter three

DEADLINES

Originally, a deadline was 'a line drawn in a military prison, by going beyond which a prisoner makes himself liable to be shot instantly' (*Chambers Etymological English Dictionary*). Nowadays it has a less draconian connotation and means simply a closing date or the point in time by which an activity has to be completed. As such it has considerable value.

> *Deadlines focus the attention and concentrate the mind. They give a clear indication of how long you have in which to get something done.*

Time limits have a similar function, but, whereas deadlines deal only with the ending of a process, time limits usually specify either starting and finishing times or the total amount of time available. In this latter respect they are similar to time frames or time slots, which really deal with the time between limits.

Time frames are usually set within a general context involving several time frames for complementary, or even competing, activities. For instance, a morning's sequence of activities – getting up, having breakfast, travelling to work, dealing with correspondence, attending a meeting, and so on – requires a series of time frames, one for each activity. If all goes well, they will be complementary and build into a picture of a reasonably trouble-free morning. But if the journey to work takes longer than anticipated or a meeting overruns, they may overlap and will therefore be competing with each other for the same period of time.

Whether you use deadlines, time limits or time frames to assist you in managing your time is, to a large extent, a matter of personal preference. Some people prefer to rely solely on a finishing time, some on a set amount of time and others on a planned sequencing of activities. There is no clear evidence favouring one technique. You must pick the one that works best for you. It may be worth trying out them all before you make your final choice. You may even decide to use all three on different occasions as determined by the particular needs of the situation.

Deadlines (or time limits or time frames) should be written down and kept in clear view. In this way, you have no excuse to offer yourself (though you may, if necessary, offer it to others, but that is another matter – just so long as you do not delude yourself) about not realising how quickly time has passed if you cannot complete the task on time. The act of writing down the deadline commits you to it. The fact of keeping it in clear view on your desk, on a notice board or inside a frequently used diary or electronic personal data assistant (PDA) is a continual reminder both of its existence and your commitment to yourself to meet it. It thus makes it much more likely that you will, in fact, achieve it.

For many activities of long duration, a deadline may be far in the future. A report may take weeks to write, a project may take months to finish, and even a simple house repair may take several weekends. In such cases, it is desirable to break the task down into stages and to set a deadline for each one. If you don't meet a sub-deadline, it shouldn't matter too much. It merely tells you that you have a little extra work to do on the next occasion. And at least it will prevent you from getting close to the deadline and then suddenly realising that you have fallen so far behind in your work that you cannot possibly hope to catch up.

If you are to achieve the time creation objective of spending less time doing things, deadlines are necessary weapons in your armoury of techniques.

Many activities cannot easily be speeded up, in terms of faster movements on your part, so it is essential to explore other ways of increasing personal efficiency. And you have to spend less time doing some things if you are to make more time for others.

In setting deadlines, you need to set them a little tighter than seems to be required, in case any unforeseen delays arise. Much of the time everything will proceed smoothly and you will find you have finished ahead of the real schedule. This is all to the good because it gives you extra time for checking over what you have done if this proves to be necessary. It is always better to finish ahead of time anyway because this helps you to avoid the intense psychological pressure which can build up if you get into the habit of running too close to deadlines. Finishing 'early' (that is, before things really must be done) helps you to remain relaxed and builds self-confidence in your own ability to cope.

You also need to avoid the greatest danger with deadlines, and that is that you may postpone an action until the last possible minute and then not be able to complete it in time. And there are other dangers. You may be over-optimistic about your own abilities and about how much can be done in a certain time. So be sure your deadlines are realistic. Or you may fail to provide for unexpected delays. By definition, it is impossible to expect the unexpected. But at least you can set a deadline which allows for some slack time, for that can always be useful.

Without deadlines, time can more easily be wasted. It is always easy to spend more time than intended over a business lunch, over telephone calls, in daydreaming and staring out of the window, or in trying to do several things at once. You can then find that you are thrashing around in total confusion and really achieving very little. You have become a headless chicken again. Greater activity is no reliable indication that useful work is being done.

Deadlines also help to overcome procrastination. There are always many plausible reasons for putting tasks, especially unpleasant or unrewarding ones, off until tomorrow. Time creation does not recognise the all-too-common philosophy that you should never put off until tomorrow what can be safely left until the day after. It is more concerned with an 'action this day' approach.

The main advantage of deadlines, however, is that they enable you to plan sensibly ahead. An orderly arrangement of activities with realistic deadlines is a very effective method on its own of ensuring greater efficiency. Allied to all the other time creation techniques and welded into an integrated approach, it begins to build into a formidable and effective approach to the better management of time both at work and in leisure.

On some occasions, you may find it useful to use a little time to check on the passage of time in activities, especially if you have identified several stages in a task and wish to check on how much time each stage is taking. You will certainly find it useful to keep a record of your progress in using deadlines, particularly of those occasions on which you fail to meet them. This will provide you with useful feedback, which will enable you to improve performance and increase your chances of becoming a laidback bear.

Chapter four

ANTICIPATORY SCANNING TECHNIQUES

It is never enough solely to attend to what is happening at the moment. Events do not exist in a vacuum. Each one is connected not only to what has already happened but also to what is about to happen.

Anticipatory scanning techniques are designed to help you to deal more speedily and effectively with whatever is about to happen. They may be defined simply as those techniques which assist you in looking ahead (physically or mentally) to try to be ready both for what is likely to happen and for probable and possible happenings with a willingness to use flexible responses to improve your ability to deal with situations.

A good example of anticipatory scanning techniques at work is to be found in the behaviour of some of the personnel on airline check-in desks. Some time ago, it was observed that those who were rated as the best check-in clerks had a habit, as they were dealing with a customer, of glancing briefly down the queue, paying particular attention to the next person in the queue and also to people who were showing visible signs of nervousness or impatience. These clerks seemed to be able to respond more quickly and more appropriately to each customer than those who concentrated solely on whoever happened to be in front of them. They were involved in far fewer altercations with passengers and generally dealt with more people in less time. Closer observations revealed that they were using these anticipatory scannings of the line of people to acquire some information that later enabled them to respond better. They smiled encouragingly at nervous passengers and helped to put them a little more at ease even before they came to deal with them. The differences in work speed and quality of performance were such that anticipatory scanning techniques now form part of the training programme for check-in personnel of at least one major international airline.

Similar behaviour can be observed every day in any good bar, where some bar staff seem to have no trouble in serving several people at once with the use of anticipatory scanning. The rest of us can develop it with a little practice. Whatever the activity, try this. Just prior to the completion of a stage of a task, glance ahead (or think ahead if it is an activity, like problem-solving, where there might not actually be anything to see) to the next stage. Don't look for all that can be seen, but pick out key features, the things that either common sense or experience tell you may cause you to vary your approach. The aim is not to try to deal with those aspects of a situation now, but simply to be ready for them when you do get to them. The signs that nervous or impatient people give of their state of mind are examples of what to look for. So are unfamiliar words and phrases in reading materials, obstacles that weren't there before on a walking or driving route, and a meeting, which follows a business lunch, at which brain-taxing matters have to be discussed.

Experience, in the form of past behaviour which was successful, can be very useful in teaching you how to tackle things in the future. In other words, never neglect the lessons of history. Having said this, remember that anticipatory scanning techniques mean you have to be more concerned with what lies ahead than with what has already been dealt with. A 'rear-view mirror' approach to life can have its uses, but priority of attention should be given to thinking ahead and to planning ahead.

Time spent planning is never wasted. A good plan can make the execution of a task very much easier by allowing you to see where you are going.

A well-planned report, for instance, makes the actual writing of it much easier. In many cases, the report will almost seem to write itself as information slots itself easily into the most appropriate place for it. Many errors and ambiguities that might otherwise intrude are avoided as a writer, having already decided how each section is to be organised, can concentrate on getting the details of written expression right.

An easy way to plan is to jot down in note form the things to be done or the items to be covered as they come to mind. They should then be studied and placed in an appropriate order of importance or the order in which they are to be tackled. In doing this, they should be grouped into stages or tasks where each one follows on logically from its predecessor. If you use an appropriate identification system (for example, lettering the parts A, B, C, D, etc. and numbering the items within each part 1, 2, 3, 4, etc.), you will have a plan in which not only is every aspect covered, but you can also see clearly which are the really important points to be dealt with.

As with any method of forecasting or predicting, it is necessary to check afterwards for accuracy. This provides useful feedback, for you will discover why any mistakes were made and will be able to avoid them in future. If you concentrate on the consequences of actions whenever you are thinking things through, this, too, will help to avoid errors later. Always be prepared for things not to work out exactly as you planned and remember what is usually called Murphy's Law: 'If things can go wrong, they will.' Careful planning will help to prevent Murphy's prophecy from coming true. Seek to identify the key features in situations and use them to help you in keeping your purpose and your direction clearly in mind. Don't let yourself be deflected from your planned course except by necessity or because a better way unexpectedly appears.

In everyday activities, a diary can help in developing anticipatory scanning techniques. You can see how a week's or a month's events relate to each other and thus be ready to respond better. Reading, especially against the clock or with a higher flow rate, helps. Going faster seems to force you to look ahead more.

There are also a number of specific activities you can practise which will develop your anticipatory scanning techniques:

1. Select a feature article from the centre pages of a newspaper. Read the first half of the article. Write down what you think the writer is going to cover in the second half. Read the second half to see how accurate your predictions were.

2. Practise skimming and previewing when reading. Always spend a few seconds glancing through material before you read it. Try to identify some of the main points or parts of the material that may cause you difficulty when you come to read them.

3. In an everyday situation such as driving a car or working through the agenda at a meeting, identify the next and the next-but-one hazard or decision to be made. Cast your mind forward briefly to them and plan how you will act. Be prepared to change if the circumstances suddenly change.

4. Try this mnemonic in your everyday activities: **PLACE**, i.e.,
   - **P**ause – stop what you are doing for a moment
   - **L**ook **A**head – cast your mind forward to the next stage or task
   - **C**ontinue – work through the next stage or task
   - **E**valuate – assess how useful looking ahead was to you

5. Question yourself about what you are going to do next and why you are going to do it in the way you are. If you can, do this aloud and record it on tape. Play it back to yourself afterwards and see if there are things which, with hindsight, you would do differently.

6. Observe others who you know are skilled performers in an activity and look for the use of anticipatory scanning techniques. Try to copy the way they do it and see how it feels.

7. Before you begin a task, write down what you are going to do and how you are going to do it. Afterwards, review your notes and see what changes you would make.

8. Press yourself to do things a little faster than you really find comfortable and see if this forces you to concentrate more and to look ahead.

9. Prepare a mental 'map' of a journey. Identify as many difficulties, obstacles and hazards as you can. Afterwards, review and see how many you were able to avoid or deal with more smoothly.

10. Take a situation in which you are not personally involved (e.g. an encounter between two people or a TV play or film). Try to 'read' how it is going to develop. Afterwards, review and assess how accurate your predictions were.

Practise some or all of these activities and see which ones appear to work best for you. These should then be added to your developing time creation strategy, so that you should then be using increased flow rates, deadlines, and anticipatory scanning techniques. Once you are happy that you have mastered these techniques, you will be ready to begin learning and applying the next one in the quest for laidback bear status.

chapter five
SELECTIVE PERCEPTION OF CUES

A cue in this context is any action, signal or event which gives an individual information about what is happening in a situation. Some cues are more important than others. For instance, if you are about to cross a road, someone waving to you from the other side is less important than the bus which is moving towards you on your own side. Usually there are too many cues for all to be perceived (or seen and understood) within a given time frame. For this reason, you have to become selective and attend to those which are of key significance at the time. The more quickly and the more accurately you can do this the better and the faster you can perform.

> *Whatever the situation, you should concentrate your attention on the key features, the highlights, or the problem areas (whichever are most relevant in the particular circumstances). By focusing on the essentials, to the exclusion of all the non-critical information available, you will be making more efficient use of your skills.*

Examples of the effectiveness of the selective perception of cues can be found in almost any area of human activity. A good driver will attend more carefully to the speed and relative positions of vehicles than to their colour or registration numbers. He or she will look for cues indicating what other road users may be about to do. Traffic lights ahead may change, young children on the kerb may unpredictably dash across the road, a dog may see another dog across the road and run to it without looking: a quick driver will spot all such potential hazards and be ready to react if the need arises. Anticipation is an important factor in the selective perception of cues.

In reading, the efficient performer will have clearly specified his or her purposes in advance, will have previewed (skimmed quickly through) the material first and will be actively looking for information rather than passively moving the eyes along the lines. This makes it possible to attend selectively to the parts that matter and so makes faster assimilation possible.

In sports, anticipation is an essential component of skilled performance, and a player has to be able to perceive selectively those cues that will enable him or her to respond before an opponent can prevent the scoring of a goal or a point. The faster such responses can be made, the better a player can become.

Even in everyday encounters with other people, a great deal of information about attitudes, motives and intentions is contained in nonverbal cues rather than in spoken words. The faster these can be identified and the more important ones responded to, the more quickly and effectively an individual can communicate.

Studies of highly skilled performers in these and other areas of activity have revealed that they actively seek cues which tell them that a situation is different from others and requires a different approach.

◆ They look for order and try to identify priorities.
◆ They look for key signposts, hierarchies of information (evidence of planning and structure).
◆ They are alert to anything that will help them to concentrate on what matters and pass over the trivial and the unimportant.

The laidback bears know what they are doing; the headless chickens are still busy but dashing around mindlessly.

Since, as has been said, there is normally too much information to be able to attend to everything, you should try to observe those cues which in effect say, 'You have to take account of us, or else.' Being able to do this helps flexible, planned performance. It allows overall for consistently greater speed.

You should try to identify priorities for your attention. Placing things in rank order with the most important at the top and the least important at the bottom helps to achieve this. Identifying, and differentiating, the important and the urgent helps too. If your car catches fire, it may be important that you rescue your briefcase but it is urgent that you yourself should escape the flames first. You can survive without your briefcase, but the alternative is no use to you at all.

It is best, once priorities have been determined, to keep to the rank order. Don't chop and change like our headless chickens. If the sequence is appropriate and you have things in the right order, everything will work out all right in any case. If you have it wrong, write it off to experience, carry on and use the lessons learned to avoid that particular mistake in future.

Practise some (or all) of the following exercises and you will find that your skill in selectively perceiving cues steadily improves:

1. Read a feature article in a newspaper. You will usually find them in the centre pages. Try to pick out the central point in the article, the main fact, idea or conclusion that the writer is seeking to communicate to the reader. Write it down. Wait 24 hours, read the article again and see if you still agree with your own assessment. If you don't, change it. If you do, you have most likely selected the main point first time round. If you can, you might also get a second opinion from someone else who has read the article.

2. Observe a street scene. On tape or in your notebook, record the key features of what you see. Then record all the other things that are happening or that are simply just there (types of buildings, road workings, people passing by, etc.). Decide how much you have ignored in focusing on the key features (most people will relegate details of buildings to the background, for instance, unless they happen to be architects). Assess how accurate you were in identifying the key features.

3. Sort the items in your in-tray into priorities. Make three piles: 'Urgent', 'Important' and 'These Can Wait'. If you have no in-tray, try simulating an in-tray exercise by imagining you have one.

4. Obtain a 'perceptual map' (one on which key buildings and other landmarks are highlighted pictorially) of a city and compare it with a traditional street map of the same area. On what basis have the key features been selected? Is a perceptual map easier to follow?

5. Why can you drive faster (within legal speed limits) on an empty straight motorway than on an empty straight single-carriageway road? List as many reasons as you can (clues: Are there more things to attend to on a motorway or fewer? Are they closer or further away? What difference does it make?).

6. Consider the cues you attend to in deciding when a joint of meat is cooked, a car is roadworthy, potatoes are ready to be picked, and that someone is being sincere.

7. When planning a holiday or a business trip, list the key factors that you take into consideration. Can you identify things you take for granted?

8. If you work in a crowded room or if you attend a party or go into the local pub, note how you can attend to one thing and exclude others, talk on the phone despite the noise or pick out one person's voice and listen to it. Ask yourself how well you can do these things. Practise one of them for a week or so and see if you notice any improvement.

9. During the Second World War, aircraft personnel were trained to spot enemy planes quickly by having silhouettes for them to identify flashed on to a screen. Practise this with silhouettes or photographs of cars from a car book. Time yourself over, say, fifty and see how much you can increase speed of identification in a week.

10. Draw a map of the route from your house to the nearest railway station or some similar destination as if for a stranger. What features and landmarks do you decide to include? How and why do you select them?

Selective perception of cues can not only speed up information processing, it can also make it more efficient by focusing on those features of a situation or sequence of events that can materially affect the outcome. As such, it is an ability which is of considerable value to the time creation student and is well worth practising by means of exercises like those above, in order to develop skill and make progress as a laidback bear.

Chapter Six

ADEQUATE INCUBATION PERIODS

At first sight it may seem that the idea of deliberately inserting into a task or activity a period of time in which nothing appears to be happening runs completely against the principles and techniques of better time creation. How does the concept of waiting time, of a period in which information is assimilated, is allowed to 'incubate' for a while, fit into a more effective approach? Is it not simply a waste of time, a device for procrastination? Part of the answer to questions like these is that, in the term 'adequate incubation periods', the emphasis is placed on the word 'adequate'. In other words, you only take the 'time out' that is necessary. If you don't provide for such periods, you do in fact waste time in less than fully productive effort. It is one of the key features that distinguish headless chickens from laidback bears. Headless chickens are so ineffective precisely because they cannot be still for a moment.

> *Adequate incubation periods are needed because there is a limit to the speed at which the brain can process information. This limit varies from person to person and most of us operate at a level well below our own potential, but it is there nonetheless and we need a technique which takes it into account.*

The periods are needed because we often take some time to form sound judgments and conclusions. Indeed, there is evidence that better conclusions are reached if adequate incubation periods are allowed. They help to avoid the stress that an over-emphasis on speed can bring. They give us time to think, to mull things over, to reflect. It is a false economy to neglect incubation periods. There will also always be occasions when the mind, like a farmer's field, has to lie fallow and be given the chance to recover for the next task. Incubation or rest periods can take several forms and all, properly used, can be of assistance in the practice of better time creation whether by managers, writers, readers, travellers or anyone else for whom speed of response is an important consideration.

The principal kind of incubation with which we shall be concerned here is the one that occurs between input and output, between preparation or planning and execution, between identifying or specifying a problem and solving it, or when the actual process of creative thinking is being carried out. It is the time during which information continues to be worked on by the brain at a level other than the conscious level. It requires no effort. All it requires is a willingness simply to put adequate incubation periods into activities and to allow them to work their particular 'magic'.

The kinds of activities in which incubation periods can play an instrumental part include problem solving, creative thinking, reading, writing, decision and judgment making, managing, forming opinions, training, learning and work planning. In later chapters we shall see specifically how some of them work, but some examples of their usefulness will not go amiss at this point.

Any rest or relaxation period in an activity can become an incubation period if, during it, what has happened previously is being considered by the brain at a level beyond the conscious and this results in a modified and improved performance when activity resumes. Any learning process needs times when, because of the effects of the learning curve, what has been learned can be mulled over ('the learning curve' in this context is a term used to refer to the fact that experience needs to be built up gradually and often cannot be forced).

◆ Other examples of incubation periods occur in situations like being able to solve a problem in a morning when it appeared insoluble the night before.

- They occur after a brainstorming session before evaluating responses obtained.

- They occur between writing a report and revising it.

- They occur between collecting information and making a decision on what to do about it.

Typically, those who are skilled in providing adequate incubation periods for themselves will make sure that they acquire all the relevant information and set aside an amount of time to give incubation a chance to occur. They will then turn their attention to some other task for a while. This might well be a task which can be completed without too much effort and without taking up too much time, bearing in mind that a desirable minimum incubation period should include an overnight wait. After this, the activity will be resumed and there is a greatly increased likelihood of confident, positive, decisive action being possible.

The benefits of such an approach are many. The main ones would appear to be that adequate incubation periods:

- boost confidence

- relax an individual

- give smoother performance of skills

- avoid errors through over-hasty judgments

- increase reliability

- avoid wasteful repetition.

This last is very important to effective time creation.

If you wish to improve your own use of these periods, you can try some or all of the following exercises:

1. Read a feature article in a newspaper. Put it to one side. Write down the main points. Then read a similar article, but this time

when you put it to one side wait for half an hour before you write down the main points. The following day, read each article again and see if you still agree with your assessment of the salient points each is making. You should find that the article with the half-hour incubation period is the one which produced the better results.

2. Select problems from a mathematics textbook or from a book which contains puzzles that provide a certain amount of intellectual challenge. One evening, attempt to solve some problems. When you encounter a problem you cannot solve, keep working at it until you can or until you have to give up. Next evening, do the same, but this time when you come to the apparently insoluble problem, make sure that you have firmly registered in your mind all the information about the problem, then go to bed. Next morning, return to the problem and see if a solution presents itself. You may have to carry out this whole experiment two or three times before you are able to form a reliable judgment, but you should find that an overnight incubation period makes it noticeably more likely that you will be able to solve the problem. Students may use homework problems for this exercise.

3. Write a letter or a report and then try to edit and polish it on the same day. Then write something, but leave it at least 24 hours before editing and polishing. You should find that the second approach produces much better results. One reason for this is the incubation period, but another is that the following day you are not so personally committed to the writing and can thus be more objective and critical in your approach to it and edit it more effectively.

4. Write a letter of complaint about something that has happened to you recently and which you feel pretty steamed up about. Put the letter to one side overnight. Do you still send it as you wrote it? Or do you tone it down a little and make it more reasoned and less abusive? The chances are you will tone it down. The incubation period has saved you from possible embarrassment by overstating your case or expecting abusiveness to work.

5. Plan an activity (for example, a journey or making a very important telephone call) and carry it out on the same day. Then do the same, but carry out the activity on the following day. Again, you should find that you get better results with fewer errors.

Where a 24 hour delay is unavailable or impracticable for a variety of reasons, try the above activities with at least a break between input and output in which a different activity is undertaken. Although the results this time may not be quite so good, you should still find that you gain some benefit from the incubation period. However, for these periods to be really useful, it is important to ensure that they are of an adequate duration. Clearly, the more you practise using them, the more accurately you will be able to see what 'adequate' means for you. Some people will need longer periods than others and all will need longer periods on some occasions. Experience in using them will enable you to become progressively better at judging the right amount of time consistent with better time creation and being a more laidback bear.

Chapter Seven
IMAGINATIVE AND INTUITIVE RESPONSES

Hard work is no substitute for talent. If you can find a way of doing something well and quickly without effort, you should take it.

> *If you can develop a kind of serendipity in being able to identify new and unusual responses to situations, you will save yourself a great deal of time and effort. Often such responses are much more effective than more conventional ones.*

If, however, you find you cannot develop such responses, even after working through this chapter, don't worry about it. As we said at the beginning of the book, not every technique described here will work for everyone. You should concentrate on developing those which work for you and ignore those that don't.

Serendipity is defined as 'the faculty of making happy chance finds'. It comes from a former name for Sri Lanka which was Serendip. In 1754, Horace Walpole coined the word from the title of a fairy tale, *The Three Princes of Serendip*, whose heroes 'were always making discoveries, by accidents and sagacity, of things they were not in quest of' (*Chambers' Etymological Dictionary*). In this context, it means being able to spot ways of doing things which add flair, style, charisma and star quality to your performance. In any activity, the truly skilled operators are not only quick and effective but also do things with that little extra flash of genius that singles them out as truly remarkable performers. This chapter, then, is for those who wish to be 'star' time creators, but it will hopefully also be of use to those who are simply concerned to improve in any way they can.

Some of what will be said here may appear to contradict advice already given. It is not meant to. But it is important to remember that differing circumstances may require differing responses. For instance, earlier the virtues of looking ahead and of planning were extolled, yet plans can have their limitations. The world record-breaking British runner, Steve Ovett, in reply to a television interviewer's question about how he planned a race, once said that he didn't. 'Once you have a plan you are vulnerable,' he said. 'You are open to attack by a competitor because you lose the flexibility to be able to respond to events.' Plans can lead to blinkered thinking. They can limit your expectations both of yourself and of others. They can restrict your ability to respond to chance events and to unexpected opportunities. They can lead to situations in which you slavishly and blindly follow your plan simply because you have one. For all these reasons and more it is important that your approach to a task should make allowance for imaginative and intuitive responses.

Such responses rely more on emotional and 'felt' reactions than on cold logical analysis. They are essentially responses which do not fit the rules or follow conventions. They can take the form of sudden insights (which often occur after an adequate incubation period has been allowed). These insights frequently produce superior solutions to problems, more appropriate responses and simple but elegant answers. They can provoke a reaction in which you say to yourself, 'Why didn't I think of that before?'

They may take the form of truly novel and creative approaches. Brainstorming, freewheeling and other divergent thinking techniques, all of which we shall encounter in due course, enable you to avoid the obvious, though there is some need for caution if using them on a problem where convergent thinking approaches are more appropriate (these are usually used when a problem is of a type likely to have a single correct answer, as with a technical or practical problem).

Instinctive reactions often produce imaginative responses. A 'gut' feeling or a sixth sense can enable you to do things without thinking. Good anticipation and being able to 'read' a situation will help, as will a sensitivity to nonverbal factors, especially in dealing with problems involving other people.

Hunches or inspired guesses can often produce reliable responses, especially in unknown situations or in mould-breaking tasks where an activity is to be performed in an entirely novel way. They can often be inevitable if you find you have a lack of relevant experience to draw upon or have to act on the spur of the moment because the situation is one that will not admit delay.

Examples of the kinds of imaginative and intuitive responses which can be generated by the above approaches are not difficult to identify. If you have ever found, or seen someone else find, a solution to a problem which is so simple you wonder why no one thought of it before, you have almost certainly witnessed an imaginative or intuitive response. Other examples include love at first sight, reactions that 'it was the right thing to do at the time' and first impressions of people. Clearly in these situations, imaginative and intuitive responses can be wrong, as can logical responses, but they are more often than not right and can be spectacularly so. For instance, a good deal of evidence now exists which shows that our first impressions of others are rarely wrong. Indeed, so infrequently are we wrong that we tend to remember vividly the occasions on which we are, thus misleading ourselves into thinking we are wrong more often.

We need these responses so that we can break free from previous habits which limit the effectiveness of our actions and so that we can make the best possible use of the resources available to us. As in the case of time creation techniques discussed in previous chapters, the benefits are many and varied, the principal one being the time that is saved when imaginative and intuitive responses are used.

These responses are most appropriate:

◆ when orthodox approaches have failed
◆ when the problem is one which demands a divergent solution,
◆ when they just *are* felt to be right
◆ when a situation is totally new.

In the main, in such circumstances the responses seem to happen of their own accord but you can encourage their use. You can encourage them simply by being ready to make an imaginative or intuitive response, or by being willing to accept the risks involved (because you know the prize may be a much better solution) or by actively looking for novelty in your responses and by resolutely refusing to get into a rut or a set pattern of action.

You can go further than this, however, and use the following exercises to stimulate your readiness and ability in making imaginative and intuitive responses:

1. Systematically break the rules of an everyday activity. For example, try acting like a stranger or a guest would act in you own home. Try smiling in a friendly – but not too friendly or leering – manner at everyone you meet. Dress differently, say, by not wearing a suit if you normally do or wearing colourful clothes if you normally wear subdued colours. You will have to be careful because other people may become hostile if you deviate too far from convention. You may, though, just find a startlingly new and refreshing way of doing something that you have previously taken for granted could not be changed.

2. Find as many uses as possible in ten minutes for a one-metre length of electrical wiring, a roll of wallpaper, a button or a ballpoint pen cap. Don't suppress ridiculous ideas and don't try to evaluate the quality or usefulness of your ideas until at least 24 hours later. You may come up with a brilliant invention.

3. Spend some of your leisure time painting or drawing, playing or listening to several different kinds of music, reading literature,

making pottery or engaging in any other creative art or craft. They will all encourage the development of the ability to make imaginative and intuitive responses.

4. Spend some time daydreaming or trying not to think of anything at all. Then tackle a problem. Does this help you to come up with a different and better approach?

5. Set out in the car with no clear destination in mind. Let yourself go where impulse takes you. Afterwards ask yourself: Wasn't that more enjoyable than a planned trip?

6. Telephone someone you have not spoken to for some time. Do it now, on impulse. Afterwards ask yourself why you chose who you did. Any regrets? You might just have revived a friendship that distance should not have been allowed to destroy. And discovered that imaginative and intuitive responses can be fun.

Headless chickens will never find the time to try things like this. They are too busy dashing around achieving nothing. It is the laidback bears who reap the rewards of the more open and creative opportunities that imaginative and intuitive responses have to offer.

Chapter Eight
CRITICAL INCIDENTS AND LEARNING PERIODS

An important element in a time creation approach is an ability to respond to changing situations and events. We have already seen something of this. Here we shall examine the contribution to be made by critical incidents and learning periods. They give an additional dimension of flexibility and we need to be ready to exploit them.

> *A critical incident may be described as a crucial event which changes the course of a person's life or, on a lesser scale, makes it easier to solve a problem. A learning period is a time which may only last for a few minutes or may last for several months, during which an individual can learn and progress most easily and productively. During such periods one is most likely to encounter, be receptive to and most readily benefit from critical incidents.*

An example of a critical incident might take the form of meeting, hearing or reading about an influential charismatic person. Or it may be a sudden revelation or insight, a shock, or a change of personal circumstances. Learning periods often occur as certain times of day are found to be better for learning and working than others.

Characteristically, skilled users of critical incidents and learning periods:

◆ Try to do their most important work at the times of day they know from experience are best for them.

◆ They exploit their failures as well as their successes, recognising that one can often learn as much, if not more, from failure as from success.

◆ They do what they can to turn circumstances to their advantage. For example, they will use a period in which they may temporarily be confined to the house by a minor ailment in order to catch up on some reading, or even to do a little writing that the presence of daily work has prevented them from tackling.

Critical incidents and learning periods compel you to re-examine and re-appraise what you have been doing.

◆ They make you propose changes and then try these changes out.

◆ Because they work in this way, they prevent you from getting into a rut and making stereotyped and repetitive responses to events.

◆ They make you self-critical, in the sense of being more aware of both your merits and your deficiencies.

◆ They stimulate your sense of curiosity and your enthusiasm.

◆ They thus have a generally beneficial and regenerative effect upon the way you look upon the world and upon your approach to the challenges it presents.

Everyone can benefit from the identification and use of critical incidents and learning periods, but they are of most value to those who feel they are in a rut. Those who have recently undergone a traumatic experience of some kind can best exploit them. They should prove particularly attractive to those who have unfulfilled ambitions and are willing to learn. They can be expected to occur when least expected. As already indicated, they should especially be looked for at your best times for working, after shocks or significant life events, after totally new experiences, and when you are in strange places that you have never previously visited.

These incidents and periods occur for many reasons. Progress in any activity and in life itself is rarely smooth and constant. It goes in spurts, followed by plateaux, and it is when you find yourself on one of these plateaux that you are more likely than usual to be ready to exploit a critical incident or a learning period.

You don't have to wait for them to occur, however.

◆ You can take steps to create the conditions in which they are most likely to occur.

◆ You can organise your activities in such a way that they recognise the 'progress – plateau – progress' approach.

◆ You can be alert during plateau periods for the next door to open.

◆ You can use plateaux for reading, research, preparation, and so on, even if there is no specific objective to latch onto.

As with other time creation techniques, you can use a number of exercises to help to stimulate your ability to develop your use of critical incidents and learning periods. Try some or all of the following exercises:

1. Select a task. Any one will do, but it should preferably be one which you usually experience some difficulty in completing. It may be studying, writing a report for work purposes, planning how to decorate a room or repair something in the house that has broken down, or it may be any other difficult task. Attempt the task at different times of day. Does any particular time of day emerge as the best time to tackle the task? If one does, you have almost certainly identified what is for you a learning period.

2. Record all the critical incidents and learning periods that you can recall having happened to you in the past. Is there any pattern in when, where, how and why they occurred? Did you make the best use of them? This exercise should help you to identify them when they occur again and perhaps make better use of them in future.

3. The next time you are blocked in an activity (that is to say, you have reached a point at which you feel you cannot make any further progress), leave it for a day or so, do something else meantime and then come back to it. Does that make it easier for

you to progress? If it does, you may have gone through an incubation period, but you may also have hit upon a learning period, especially if you select a time of day when you know from experience you can work better.

4. Set aside some time each week for reading you would not otherwise do. This encourages a learning orientation and a general receptiveness to new information and ideas. It makes for a developing open-mindedness that will enable you to exploit future critical incidents and learning periods to the full.

5. Go to a public meeting to listen to someone you know or have heard is a good speaker. Afterwards, is there any urge on your part to 'do something' about the subject of the speech? If there is, you have almost certainly experienced a critical incident.

6. Make sure that you meet and talk at some length to at least one new person each week. Doing this will have a similar effect to general reading. It makes you more receptive to new information, experience and ideas.

7. Change your sleeping habits for a week. If you usually go to bed late and rise late, try going to bed early and rising early. If you usually go to bed early, try going to bed late and rising late. Keep as detailed a record as you can of the effects upon your working habits and patterns. It is just possible that you may be able to identify a better way of organising your life. It is surprising how many people find working very late at night or very early in the morning effective. But not both in the same week, of course, as everyone needs a reasonable amount of sleep.

8. Try reading some inspirational works. You can choose religious or philosophical books as you prefer. Some possible writers are Marcus Aurelius, La Rochefoucauld and Mao Tse-tung, but you may prefer the Bible, the Koran or the writings of the Buddha, especially if you have not read them before. You may well find that one or other of these provides you with the possibility of experiencing a critical incident.

These exercises will help to promote your ability to develop this particular aspect of time creation, but you will need at all times to keep your mind open to the possibility of critical incidents and learning periods occurring. They can do a lot to make life easier, as well as more productive. And laidback bears like to achieve both of these.

Chapter Nine
TIMING AND SYNCHRONISATION

If you are to be fully successful in using time creation techniques, you will need to develop your sense of timing and your ability to synchronise activities. Things need to be done not only at the right time for doing them but also at a time which fits in with whatever else has to be done.

Timing and synchronisation are therefore important considerations as they help in the process of knowing when to speed up and when to slow down. In enabling this to happen, they can contribute both to increasing overall speed and to the saving of time.

Timing is almost an art – more than doing the right thing at the right time – and has much in common with the concept of serendipity discussed earlier. It is that quality of being able to judge precisely the right moment at which to act. It is a concept which comedians understand very well, for they know that if they do not deliver the punch line at exactly the right time the audience may not laugh. Synchronisation is concerned with fitting actions together without overlap. Such dovetailing enables actions to be timed for maximum effect, avoiding cutting across others in discussions and thus achieving smooth changeovers from one activity to another.

Developed timing and synchronisation are evidenced:

◆ in the existence of time slots
◆ in the ability to accommodate overrunning of an activity without overlap by being flexible

- in changeovers between speakers in conversations, discussions and meetings
- in moving smoothly from one stage of a task to another
- in timetables and programming
- in critical paths
- in schedules and diaries
- in all kinds of rhythms and activity patterns.

Skilled users of timing and synchronisation as techniques:

- exhibit smoother performance
- make fewer errors
- are more relaxed and confident
- waste less time
- make generally faster movements
- are responded to more favourably by others because they interact more skilfully
- exploit opportunities for effective action because their developed sense of timing helps them to identify an opportunity before others realise it is there.

To exploit timing and synchronisation to the full, it is necessary to be able to identify the ends of tasks and stages within tasks, to recognise pauses and natural breaks in activities and to be able to sense what it is appropriate to do at any particular moment in time. Good anticipation skills are therefore also necessary, as is a preparedness to make use of sudden and unexpected opportunities for action. A sensitivity to what others are doing and how they will react helps timing and synchronisation to be used more effectively. Other time creation techniques, such as anticipatory scanning and selective perception of cues naturally have an additional contribution to make that is very important. From what has been said, a number of benefits of timing and synchronisation can be identified. As well as enabling unexpected chances to be exploited, they provide a useful supplement to other techniques by saving wasted time, reducing costs (for example, by timing telephone calls where appropriate), increasing interpersonal effectiveness and enabling more than one activity at a time to be managed. In serving the public, for instance, as a bar person, they help in the process of being able to take one person's order, serve another and give change to a third, all at the same time.

Apart from those in public-contact occupations, better timing and synchronisation are important to speakers, participants in meetings and negotiations, travellers, students, house managers, cooks, factory supervisors, politicians, organisers of various kinds, broadcasters, engineers, architects, lawyers and secretaries. Indeed, as with other time creation techniques, it is difficult to think of a group of people who could not benefit in some way from better timing and synchronisation. And the headless chickens among us can benefit most of all.

We shall go into more detail later over when to speed up and when to slow down, but no consideration of timing and synchronisation can be complete without at least a brief look at acceleration and deceleration in activities. Generally speaking, speed is controlled first of all by the rate of information flow. When there is a lot of information to process, that is, when the information density is high, it is necessary to slow down. When the information density is low, it becomes easier to speed up. A serious time creator will make sure that speed is increased to the maximum when information density drops. He or she will also exploit timing skills when plans have to be varied for whatever reason and will exploit synchronisation skills in situations such as when distances between people involve time differences, in planning campaigns or when organising events.

There are at least three ways in which all of these aspects of timing and synchronisation can be developed. Firstly, you can observe people whom you have previously identified as being skilled in this aspect of time creation. From this simple activity much can be learned. Secondly, you can reflect on your own experience and learn from that. Thirdly, you can learn by practising with exercises and experiments like the following:

1. Observe a comedian on a TV programme. Study his or her timing, the waiting for laughter to die down but not out, the pacing of jokes and the delivering of punch lines. Are there any lessons from these observations which you can apply in your own work? If you have to attend meetings, make after-dinner speeches or go to conferences and conventions, you should find some at least that you can use.

2. Attend a meeting or discussion. Observe how the contributors synchronise with each other. Note the reactions to talking across others or interruptions. Note the role of the person in the chair and the cues (most of them nonverbal) which are used when synchronising. You should find, for instance, that when a person is about to speak, he or she will try to establish eye contact with the chair. Some of the more interesting cues to be observed are those to show disapproval when one person talks across or interrupts someone else.

3. Study someone who is preparing a meal. How are the various activities synchronised? What is the critical path (that is, the sequence of main events which must be done in order and usually to a schedule with time limits)? When and how do errors occur? How is activity overload (that is, trying to do too many things at once) avoided?

4. Plan an event (a party, a fete, a conference or a wedding). What synchronisation problems arise? How crucial is timing and at which points? How do you allow for the plan to go wrong and what kind of contingency provisions do you have to make?

5. Plan your diary for the week ahead so as to make the best use of every time slot. What can be done to overcome and resolve competing claims upon your time? How will you fill 'downtime' (that is, any time during which, for whatever reason, you are unable to proceed with your planned activities)?

6. Plan a holiday. Study as you do so the timing implications (for

example, arriving just after the carnival has finished or when the weather is poor). Study also the synchronisation implications (for example, sorting out railway or airline timetables). What solutions can you devise for the problems that do arise?

7. Watch a TV discussion with the sound off. What kinds of nonverbal signals are given by the participants to manage timing and synchronisation? Are there any that you may be able to use in your own encounters with other people?

Trying these exercises and experiments should help to convince you that a sense of timing and an ability to synchronise activities can make a significant contribution to the effective use of time creation techniques. You will have taken yet another step towards building a more effective strategy for both keeping up with the pace of change and for creating time for yourself. You will have moved further forward in your own metamorphosis from headless chicken to laidback bear.

Chapter Ten

SLIPPAGE AND DOWNTIME

One of the facts of life is that things never run smoothly. There is always some spare time, which usually comes in small amounts, but small amounts can quickly add up to something much larger. It is easy to waste this time unless you plan for it. Provisions for dealing with slippage and downtime are therefore important to effective time creation. Many of the reasons for planning ahead are obvious. For instance, illnesses can always occur, and usually do so unexpectedly, so we need to have contingency arrangements to deal with them. When travelling, delays these days are becoming increasingly common for a variety of reasons, quite apart from the disrupting effects of breakdowns and hold-ups. The headless chicken dashes around in a panic at such moments, but the laidback bear is ready for them.

Slippage or 'uptime' occurs when things do not take as long as you expected they would. Perhaps you had help from an unexpected quarter or maybe your timing was better than normal. Downtime is when you cannot continue because something beyond your control prevents you from progressing: perhaps a key person is late for a meeting because of traffic problems or you cannot speak to someone on the telephone because their number is constantly engaged.

Other examples are when fewer letters arrive in the morning mail than usual or you have fewer emails to deal with or fewer appointments for the day. If you go to see people and they have not yet returned from one of their own appointments or they are out for some other reason, this gives you slippage. If a train you intend to catch is cancelled, this creates downtime which affects you and everyone else who was going to travel on it. If you make a journey in your car and the car breaks down, this means further downtime. Or if you are on a bus and the traffic is lighter than usual, you have more uptime. At the worst, you break a leg and then you have a mountain of downtime to deal with.

One of the characteristics of skilled users of slippage and downtime is that they always have something to do to keep their mind occupied, they are never bored and can easily switch from one thing to another. They keep relaxed but busy. They do not get in a frenzy and do not get hassled and harassed, yet they get things done. They are laidback bears rather than headless chickens.

We are all familiar with Murphy's Law which was referred to earlier and holds that if it is possible for things to go wrong then sooner or later they will. Social entropy (the tendency for events to degenerate into chaos) afflicts us all. There will always be factors which work to create times in which you cannot do what you intended. So you might as well provide for them.

There are benefits to be derived from providing in advance for slippage and downtime. It gives you a more efficient time use, more gets done in the end, there is more variety of activity. You can also, of course, use these periods for thinking or relaxing, for reading, for listening to music and a thousand other things.

The ones who have the most to gain from a better use of slippage and downtime are those who feel that they never have enough time in a day to get everything done. But anyone who works for a living can benefit. Anyone who relies on public transport will have ample opportunities for doing many things which might not otherwise get done. Shift workers often have extra opportunities because they work at times when everyone else is asleep and they can work uninterrupted.

You can begin to exploit your own slippage and downtime right away. Take a close look at your last week. How much time was wasted? Why was this so? What could have been done in each of your periods of slippage and downtime? If you cannot remember the last week too well, set aside this week for recording these periods. Record the activity, what you intended to do, how you were prevented, for how long, and what you do with the time.

If you are going to develop your use of slippage and downtime, you need a reserve bank of activities of a kind that can be undertaken easily and without delay. You should also observe what other people do with their slippage and downtime. You should try some or all of the following exercises and experiments:

1. Make a list of ten activities that typically take you the following time slots – 5 minutes, 10 minutes, 30 minutes and 1 hour. Over a week, see how many you can complete without undue trouble in your slippage and downtime.

2. List the 10 activities or tasks that you never seem to get around to. Over a week, see how many you can fit into your slippage and downtime. Which are the easiest to fit in and which are the hardest?

3. List some occasions when events have not gone successfully for reasons beyond your control and you have been left with time on your hands. How far would planning ahead for slippage and downtime have helped?

4. Observe what happens on TV when a news or feature item breaks down or there are other technical difficulties. How is the time occupied? Are there any differences between national and regional television?

5. List ten books you want to read but never seem to have the time. See how many you can read in your slack time in a month.

6. Consider whether in your own activities it is possible deliberately to create slippage and downtime. What do you think are the advantages of doing this? Some would argue that it creates time for yourself, it gives variety and prevents a person from becoming a workaholic? Do you agree?

7. List the ways in which you waste time when you know in your heart that there are things you could easily and usefully be doing.

Now identify a solution that works for you for each situation and put these solutions into practice.

Using slippage and downtime is yet another tool you can use to improve your time creation skills. It takes up slack without adding to the strain. The aim is not to be working all the time, merely to be occupied and active in a relaxed manner rather then frantically dashing about trying to get things done against all the odds; to be a laidback bear rather then a headless chicken.

Chapter Eleven

FLEXIBLE PERFORMANCE STRATEGIES

Generally speaking, things are done better when they are done systematically rather than haphazardly or by rule of thumb.

> *Systematic approaches to tasks enable us to avoid wasteful trial-and-error methods, and enable us to reduce the effects of chance happenings upon activities through building into an approach a degree of flexibility to anticipate the unexpected.*

Activities which are handled in this way will thus usually be more successful than those that are treated intuitively. This may not always be the case, but more often than not it will. Walk into a situation unprepared, without having thought about it much beforehand and without a method for dealing with what you encounter, and you are more likely to make mistakes, to miss opportunities and to overlook things which really ought to be attended to than you are if you have prepared, have thought about what might happen and have a system for dealing with whatever confronts you.

Before tasks can be tackled with any hope of success, they need to be organised. This means that you have to think about them and try to identify stages and even sub-stages which combine together to make up the task as a whole. It is useful, in doing this, to try to see tasks in terms of beginnings (how do you start?), middles (how do you deal with the main part of a task?) and ends (how do you finish the task off and know that you have not overlooked any aspect of it that is significant?). In other words, there is a kind of Rule of Three in task analysis. It is usually convenient to break an activity down into these three parts. Sometimes you may feel it is necessary to break it into more than three, but it will rarely be appropriate to break it into fewer than three.

Most tasks can be analysed logically in this way. They have their own natural internal sequencing and there will be certain things that must be done before others and some that will have to be done after. In carrying out task analysis, there are several available methods of ordering and arranging activities. The stages into which tasks can be broken down can be arrived at in a number of ways.

1. Some will have chronological staging. That is, the activities are such that they must be carried out in a strict time sequence. An example of this might be organising a conference or even arranging the games and other activities for a children's party. In a conference, you can't have the closing speech before the opening or dinner before lunch. At a party, you can't have the jelly and custard before the sandwiches (or – knowing children – can you?) and it's advisable to get all the most energetic games over before tea (unless you like attending to sick children).

2. Some tasks are best dealt with if the most important parts are tackled first as, for instance, when dealing with your in-tray in a morning. It can be helpful here to distinguish between what is important and what is urgent, so that the latter can be given priority. Others are best approached by seeing to the minor aspects first and leaving the most important until the last, as in organising a concert in which the 'stars' appear at the end or when scheduling a factory awards ceremony.

3. In some activities you move gradually from the known to the unknown. This happens in the organisation of training programmes for employees and in dealing with an in-tray in which routine items are mixed with new or one-off items, all of more or less equal importance. In other activities you might deal with the unknown first and then move on to the familiar, as in revising for an examination or going through papers in preparation for a meeting.

4. You may begin with the general and move on to the particular, or vice versa. You may even deal with things by areas or aspects of a subject.

The main requirement of whichever method, or combination of methods, is used is that it should be appropriate to the nature of the task.

The next move, once the task has been analysed, is to use a strategy which comprises a series of systematically operated steps for dealing with the situation. This must not, however, be applied rigidly. A degree of flexibility to allow for unforeseen events or any unpredictability at any point in the task is essential, so that what we are looking for here are flexible performance strategies.

One such strategy, which we encountered very briefly earlier and which has a wide range of applications, has the mnemonic title PAPA–ROMEO–OSCAR and is also known as the PRO Approach. It can be represented diagrammatically as follows:

ACTION TO TAKE	STEP	SUB-STEP	QUESTIONS TO ASK
Performance Analysis (Initial) (**PA**)	1. **R**eview		Where am I?
	2. **O**bjectives (general)		Where do I want to go?
	3. **M**ethods	**O**bjectives (specific) **S**kills **C**ontexts **A**ttitudes **R**esources	How will I get there?
Performance Analysis (Final) (**PA**)	4. **E**valuation		How will I know I've arrived?
	5. **O**ngoing		Where will I go next?

Hence: **PAPA – ROMEO – OSCAR**

The strategy can be used, for example, as a basis for guiding a self-development programme or for a simple activity such as a journey to a new destination. The questions on the right are designed to show how simple the strategy is in essence, but some further brief explanation of the key words used in this five-step strategy might be helpful. Let's try it on the two examples – a self-development programme and a journey.

◆ The first step, **Review**, as its title implies, is concerned with making an assessment of the situation as you find it at the beginning of the activity. In self-development it calls for an analysis of your performance in the activity/skill to be developed. For a journey, it means identifying the starting point.

◆ The second step, **Objectives** (general), is the point at which you determine your main intentions for self-development or the general destination (for example, the town) for a journey.

◆ The third step, **Methods**, requires you to decide how the self-development is to be achieved or how the journey is to be made. The sub-step here suggests some points to consider in making this decision. Not all of them will be relevant on every occasion, however. You should only consider those that will help. What are your specific **Objectives** (for example, the precise address of your destination)? What **Skills** will you need to exercise in achieving your objectives (driving a car, perhaps)? In what **Context** is the activity taking place (the journey is part of a holiday tour, say)? What is your **Attitude** to the activity (you are looking forward to it)? What **Resources** do you need for its successful completion (car, petrol, road map, etc.)?

◆ The fourth step, **Evaluation**, is undertaken at the end of the activity. You would conduct a similar performance analysis to that conducted in the Review step and determine how far your self-development had succeeded or whether the journey had been made satisfactorily.

◆ The last step, **Ongoing**, presents the opportunity to learn from mistakes made and identified, and to decide the next area for self-development or the next journey to be made. The process as a whole can thus either end here or be repeated, depending on whether or not you feel you have got to where you want to be. This would apply to both the examples used here, self-development or a journey. And they are only examples. As stated earlier, the approach can be applied to many different kinds of activities.

Throughout the process you should bear in mind the need to be flexible and to change your approach if necessary. One aspect where this is particularly true is in regard to speed. The Rule of Three can be applied to this as well. Think of your 'gears' in speed as being high, medium and low. On a journey, there will be times when each one will either be appropriate or may be forced upon you (you cannot drive at high speed in dense traffic and will have to drive slowly). In self-development, there will be times when progress can be quick and others when it can only be slow.

The aim in using a flexible performance strategy should be to operate at the optimum speed and in the optimum way for the conditions and circumstances applying at the time. The more closely this can be achieved, the more efficiently you will be using your time, and the more effective your overall performance is likely to be. And the closer you will approach to being a truly laidback bear.

Chapter Twelve

CRITICAL ANALYSIS OF PERFORMANCE

There is one more major technique of time creation which we need to use in order to complete our repertoire. Reasonably regularly, about every six months, we need to stand back and review what we have done and assess what we have achieved. We need to carry out a critical analysis of performance up to that point.

For such a review, we need a systematic approach that is easy to learn and easy to begin practising. It is necessary so that we can be confident that we have indeed made progress and can see what we need to do next. If we have not made progress, we need to know why and to try to identify ways of remedying the situation.

> *Being critical, in the sense in which the word is used here, implies looking for points of merit as well as for faults. It is not meant to be used in the popular definition of the word to look only for faults. It therefore involves reaching a balanced judgment of events that can be defended by rational argument and the use of evidence.*

The approach offered here consists of the following:

◆ What has been done is considered from three main standpoints: **Content**, **Intentions** and **Treatment**. On the basis of the responses to these, an **Evaluation** of events is arrived at. This gives us a convenient mnemonic: **CITE**.

◆ The **Content**, in this context, is what has actually been done within the set time period. It represents an attempt to state explicitly what it is precisely that has been done. Thus, this stage is purely factual and contains no opinions.

◆ The **Intentions** are the reasons why the actions have been taken in the first place. An attempt needs to be made to ascertain whether the aims were reasonable and achievable, and whether or not they fitted well into the overall approach to better time creation. If the intentions were too ambitious or flawed for some other reason, this is the time to be honest with oneself and admit to having tried to do too much.

◆ The **Treatment** calls for a concern with how the events being studied took place. An assessment is required of the techniques used, the method of selecting the objectives for achievement and the actual way in which things were tackled.

◆ The **Evaluation** is based on the three above factors and involves reaching conclusions and judgments about the facts that can be supported by evidence and defended in argument. It also requires suggesting how, where and why failures occurred and how deficiencies can be remedied. It should emphasise, however, the achievements made, since to focus too heavily on failure may well deter an individual from continuing to use the method.

The following checklist may be helpful in carrying out the process:

1. **Content:** What, precisely, are the facts about what has been done so far to achieve better time creation? Are they accurate, as far as I can tell? Are they plausible? How reliable are the facts?

2. **Intentions:** What were you trying to achieve? Were your objectives reasonable or were you trying to do too much within the time period?

3. **Treatment:** Was this a rational approach? Have you tried to make things look better than they were in any way? Have you underestimated your achievements in any way? Could you have done anything differently and been more effective?

4. **Evaluation:**If you failed to achieve your objectives, how, why and in which parts or ways did you fail? In which parts did you do particularly well? What is your final overall judgment, bearing in mind your responses to all the foregoing points?

You would not necessarily ask all these questions every time. There are times when other questions would be more appropriate. These are really only intended to get you thinking critically about what you do.

An alternative approach you may prefer is the one we encountered in Part 1 Chapter 11 as a flexible performance strategy. This would, in this context, work as follows:

Review	**P**erformance **A**nalysis	**O**bjectives (specific)
Objectives (general)		**S**kills
Methods		**C**ontexts
Evaluation	**P**erformance **A**nalysis	**A**ttitudes
Ongoing		**R**esources

Key:

Review	Critical analysis (see method above)
Objectives (general)	A general statement of intentions expressed as results to be achieved
Methods	A factual statement of how you did what you did
Evaluation	Forming conclusions and judgments about failure and success
Ongoing	What you are going to do in the next time period
Objectives (specific)	A detailed statement with specific quantifiable targets or goals
Skills	The abilities you need to achieve your targets or goals
Contexts	The situations in which you have to operate, be they work or leisure or both
Attitudes	A statement of your attitudes to achieving better time creation
Resources	What you will need in order to achieve your targets or goals

Performance **A**nalysis   The process described earlier, seen as part of the Review process

Whichever method you choose, you should now have acquired all the necessary skills to complete the transformation from headless chicken to laidback bear.

Part Two:
Overcoming Problems in Using Time Creation Techniques

Aspects of the use of time creation techniques are considered from the point of view of the problems that can arise, and solutions are suggested for each of them. This Part should be of particular interest to those headless chickens who are sceptical of being able to change their ways to any significant extent in their quest to become laidback bears.

Chapter Thirteen
ELIMINATION OF FAULTS

Most of the faults, errors and mistakes in the use of more effective time creation techniques stem from the inadequate use or downright misuse of the techniques, particularly by the headless chickens among us. We can extract the main points made in each of the chapters of Part 1 of this book and identify faults which need to be remedied. We can also suggest simple solutions for each one.

The following table lists concisely the principal faults of which headless chickens are guilty, and alongside gives the laidback bear's solution in each case:

Headless Chicken's Fault	Laidback Bear's Remedy
Forgets to record feedback or neglects to record it altogether, in the mistaken belief that it really is not necessary.	Recognises the vital nature of accurate feedback if you are to know how much progress you are making and in which areas.
Makes careless errors in recording feedback when he or she does remember to record it.	Checks for errors before moving on to the next task.
Leaves gaps in records of feedback so that an incomplete picture emerges.	Ensures the records are comprehensive as well as accurate.
Cannot adapt flow rates to suit the circumstances and is always dashing around.	Adapts the flow rate to the nature of the task and the degree of urgency.
Keeps going back to worry over things already done when there is no need.	Recognises that when a task is done it is done.

Headless Chicken's Fault	Laidback Bear's Remedy
Ignores deadlines until it is too late to complete the work on time, and thus becomes a victim of artificial urgency or leaving things until undue haste is inevitable.	Keeps an eye on deadlines so that he or she does not become a victim of unnecessary or artificial urgency.
Does not bother to set mini-deadlines for intermediate parts of a task to give better control.	Sets mini-deadlines as appropriate to be able to see when stages within stages have to be completed.
Makes no or very little use of anticipatory scanning techniques.	Keeps looking and thinking ahead periodically, to be ready for upcoming changes in the nature of the task.
Cannot distinguish the unimportant from the important and thus every task is urgent.	Sets priorities which separate the important from the urgent from the unimportant from the routine.
No prioritisation of activities.	Sets priorities and concentrates his or her efforts on the most important ones.
Does not use incubation periods to let things mull over and cannot relax; has to be on the move all the time and confuses activity for achievement.	Incubates at appropriate points in the task and makes sure that regular provision is made for relaxation and recreation.
Does not make use of imaginative and intuitive responses.	Is always on the lookout for unusual or insightful ways of doing things.
Ignores critical incidents and learning periods, and has no best times for activities.	Knows when he or she is at his or her best and times activities when possible for the most productive times.
Feels that everything has to be done now.	Recognises that you cannot do everything at once, nor can you do more than is reasonable.

Headless Chicken's Fault	Laidback Bear's Remedy
Has poor timing and does not proceed through tasks smoothly and confidently.	Recognises the importance of timing and avoids interruptions to important activities where possible.
Cannot synchronise or dovetail activities.	Continuously seeks to improve and develop synchronisation and dovetailing skills.
Gets frustrated by slippage and downtime.	Recognises these are inevitable and prepares for their occurrence.
Has no reserve bank of activities.	Always has other tasks to get on with when delays are inevitable or beyond control.
Has no strategies for performance.	Develops flexible performance strategies for a wide range of situations.
Lacks flexibility.	Is always prepared to change to meet changed circumstances.
Fails to analyse performance.	Sets aside time periodically to review and assess performance and look for ways of improving.
Lacks a method for evaluation.	Either uses one of the methods outlined above in Part A Chapter 12 or develops one to suit.
Takes on more than can reasonably be done by one person.	Whittles out unnecessary tasks to keep the workload to a reasonable level.
Unable to say, 'No'.	Has learned to say, 'No' politely but firmly.

Chapter fourteen

MOTIVATION

If you are to change yourself from a headless chicken to a laidback bear, you have to be motivated to do it. You need to be convinced of the desirability of self-motivation. This chapter should help you to achieve this. You may also want to motivate others, perhaps family members or workmates. This chapter should help you to achieve this as well.

Better motivation will encourage faster and better use of the techniques you learned in Part 1 of this book. It will help you to get action now and to avoid procrastination.

Analysis of the process of motivation suggests four things that you can do to improve your ability to motivate yourself and others.

Firstly, try to understand what your needs are or the needs of your subordinates in terms of security, social esteem, self-fulfilment:

1. Find out not only what you or they need but also what you or they want. You may not be able to achieve it easily, if at all, but you might at least be able to modify your approach to motivation in the light of this knowledge.

2. Use financial rewards as a prime motivator. Money is important because it satisfies so many needs. It provides what people want to increase their standard of living, but it also serves as the most effective way of recognising achievement (self-fulfilment) and enabling people to demonstrate their achievement to others (social esteem).

3. Bear in mind, however, that money is not the only reward that people need and want. They can also be motivated by recognition,

praise, promotion and the work itself through the opportunity to achieve something extra or to take on greater responsibility. This sort of reward can sometimes be more effective than money. It depends on individual needs and the reason you should try to identify those needs, in yourself and others is that you can then be more discriminating in the use of rewards.

Secondly, remember the importance of expectations as an influence on motivation. A reward will be much more effective when people know what they can get if they work hard and well enough. You should therefore:

1. Ensure that the relationship between effort and reward is clearly defined in any financial reward system.

2. Set targets and standards which are achievable, but not too easily.

3. Make yourself and others aware that achievements will be recognised by praise, a special reward or the opportunity to do better. Do not cheapen the reward. Give praise only when it is due.

4. Make it known, as far as possible, what you or other people have to do to gain promotion or take on greater responsibility.

5. Spell out not only what you or they can get if they do well but also what you or they will not get if they do badly. This is not intended to be a crude carrot-and-stick tactic but a clarification of the fact that what people achieve or do not achieve is up to them.

Thirdly, if you are mainly concerned with motivating others and persuading them to adopt a laidback bear approach, you should always keep in mind that your aim is the creation of conditions such that people can achieve their own goals best by directing their efforts towards the success of the enterprise. Hence the value of:

1. Identifying people's needs, so that you can try to adjust rewards to meet those needs.

2. Getting people to think for themselves about what they can and should do, and agreeing targets and standards with them.

3. Recognising the fact that people can be motivated by the work itself if it satisfies their needs for responsibility and achievement. Do this by using the following job-enrichment techniques:

   ◆ increasing the responsibility of individuals
   ◆ giving people more scope to vary the methods, sequence and pace of their work
   ◆ giving a person or group a complete natural unit of work, thus reducing specialisation
   ◆ removing some controls from above, while ensuring that individuals or groups are clearly accountable for achieving defined targets or standards
   ◆ giving people the control information needed to monitor their own performance
   ◆ encouraging the participation of employees in planning work and innovating techniques
   ◆ assigning projects to individuals or groups which give them more responsibility and help them to increase their expertise.

Lastly, remember that group pressures can affect motivation, for good or ill. Take steps to get groups on your side by involving them in key decisions which affect their work.

Chapter Fifteen

CONTINUATION AND FOLLOW-UP

Clearly there is little point in working through a book like this unless you are prepared to continue practising the techniques you have learned. You should, therefore, keep practising for the next few weeks at least.

◆ It is best if you can find some time each day for practice. How much time you spend on this practice is for you to decide. Thirty minutes will probably suit most people. If you set aside a longer amount of time, there is the risk that you will find reasons for not practising on those days when you have been particularly busy with other matters.

◆ Keep a record of your progress in this practice. As has been stressed previously, accurate feedback is essential at all times if you are really to know how well you are doing and where the areas are that need special attention to bring them up to scratch.

◆ Find some time each month to review some of the less well-remembered parts of this book. You may well be able to identifying new ways of bringing about improvements.

◆ Make periodic checks on your performance in the key areas discussed in Part 1. Any deficiencies can then be remedied at an early stage and prevent you backsliding into being a headless chicken.

◆ Every year, check through the book as a whole to see if you need to brush up on any points. This need not take long, a few minutes at most if you have been practising what you have learned.

Follow-up tests, if you wish to use them to introduce some variety into your continuation procedures, might take the form of asking yourself how headless chickens and laidback bears would act differently in various situations. Some examples might include dealing with an in-tray, finding there are more things to be done than time in which to do them, and responding to requests for assistance from colleagues when you already have a full schedule. You might like to make entries in your diary for the dates when you will tackle a follow-up exercise. Three months, six months and one year from now should be worth considering.

The main point is to keep the idea of improvement in mind all the time. Do not let yourself fall into the complacent trap of thinking that your achievements at the end of working through this book represent a final picture. In some respects, you will have only just begun to tackle the problems of improvement and may still need to watch for any tendency to revert to being a headless chicken.

Chapter Sixteen
RISK TAKING

In your quest to keep pace with the increasing speed of modern life without dashing about, you may be tempted to take certain short cuts with the advice contained in this book. If too recklessly undertaken, this could be dangerous and return you to headless chicken status overnight. There are, however, some sensible short cuts that you can take and still feel that you have given matters the care and attention they need and deserve. Let us look at each of the basic time creation techniques outlined in Part 1 in turn and see where and how this may be possible.

Feedback should be obtained fairly frequently at first, but once you have got the hang of a particular technique and simply want to keep an eye on things to make sure performance does not deteriorate through complacency, you can reduce the frequency. The important point is to keep a record of all the feedback you do obtain, because this is the only way you can look back and spot precisely where things started to go wrong, if indeed this is the case. It is far easier to deal with specific errors than to remedy a general feeling of unease.

When you are increasing **flow rates**, make sure that you do it gradually at first until your performance meets the level you require. You can then experiment with faster speeds, which are a kind of short cut to getting things done, secure in the knowledge that if you have to go back to the previous flow rate you are still acting faster than you were at the beginning of the process of acquiring these new skills.

Not everyone sticks to every **deadline** they have set themselves. They are mainly there to prompt you to take action. Try to beat a deadline if you can, as this can be a very useful short cut to the next activity. You may even find that, if you have identified mini-deadlines to work to, that you can skip quickly over some of them or even omit them altogether without loss. There is little point in sticking to a plan simply because it is there, if you can see a faster way to completion.

At first, mainly because they are new to many people, more time is spent on **anticipatory scanning techniques** than is necessary. The idea is to get a quick impression of the task ahead and not to go into detail about how to tackle it. A few seconds should be all that is required. If it takes longer than this, you may be trying to do things which are dealt with in the next three paragraphs below.

With **selective perception of cues** it is important to concentrate on what are truly the important features of a situation. You are looking to identify the highlights, the salient points, the things which you simply cannot afford to ignore. There is no point in including something simply because it might become important later on. Your flexible performance strategies (see below) should take care of that. The rest you can skip over with a reasonably easy conscience, knowing that anything missed by one technique will almost certainly be covered by another.

Adequate incubation periods can be shortened to save time, but be careful to ensure that you have correctly identified the ones that require an overnight pause. They cannot be reduced if they are to work properly. To curtail those would be to take a risk not worth taking. You also need to be careful about cutting down on incubation periods when you are learning something new and it is important for you to get it right.

It is difficult to take short cuts with **intuitive and imaginative responses** simply because by their very nature you have no way of knowing when they are likely to occur. Sometimes, however, when a brilliant idea about how to tackle a task springs to mind out of the blue, you do not need to act upon it there and then. Simply make a brief note of it, but in enough detail so that you will later recall exactly what it was you intended to do, and this will provide a useful and safe short cut.

A similar problem arises with **critical incidents and learning periods**. You can save some time by noting the insight for later action, but very often it will be best to exploit to the full the incident or period whenever it occurs.

Timing and synchronisation present perhaps the best opportunities for taking sensible short cuts. Very often when people speed up and then encounter a difficulty which forces them to slow down, they forget to speed up again once the problem is passed. You should be continuously on the lookout for opportunities to speed up so that you can operate, if you like, at the level of the highest common factor in a task rather than the lowest common denominator.

Slippage and downtime offer the chance to examine a task and ask whether it needs to be done at all. If you find you are continually being prevented from doing something by forces or events beyond your control, perhaps you should at least be looking for an alternative route to where you want to be. For instance, if you have difficulty in reaching people on the telephone, it might be more effective and quicker to email them.

Flexible performance strategies, as we said above, help to ensure that your short cuts do not lead to more problems than they solve. It is important to keep your strategies flexible. The last thing you want to do is to become set in your ways. Once you have successfully dealt with a situation in a certain way, there is a great temptation to tackle all subsequent similar problems in the same way. This can be a very quick road back to headless chickendom if you are not careful.

Critical analysis of performance, which you only engage in in any depth at the end of a cycle of activity, may not offer many short cuts itself, but it may lead to the identification of other shortcuts available in the use of other techniques. Always be on the lookout for anything that will give you a faster and better performance without endangering your status as a laidback bear.

Chapter Seventeen
VIGILANCE AND ATTENTION

It is very easy when you are learning and developing new techniques to take your eye off the ball, as it were. You need to guard against this. In particular, you should be watching for any tendency on your part to procrastinate or to take the view, 'Why leave until tomorrow what I can safely leave until the day after?' You should also be looking for any backsliding into old headless-chicken habits.

No one can do this for you. You have to maintain your focus on your ultimate objectives and not be distracted from them. Your attentiveness to carrying out all the guidance and advice you are given in this book will determine how successful you have been in transforming yourself into a laidback bear who copes with everything without strain or stress or panic.

> *If you have difficulty concentrating on a task, try reminding yourself of your original purpose. The more detailed you can make this, the better. Everyone has a limit to the length of his or her span of concentration. If yours is not up to the demands you are required to make upon it, try breaking tasks up into manageable stages to enable you to maintain progress.*

Maintaining effectiveness and efficiency are easier if you are alert to the possibilities of things going wrong and if your attention is given fully to the task in hand.

Other ways of maintaining good levels of concentration, and therefore of performance, are:

1. Spend a little more time on obtaining **feedback**, but bear in mind what you have already learned about this.

2. Increase the **flow rate** slightly, just enough to put a little extra pressure on yourself, but not so much as to make the cure worse than the disease.

3. Stick more closely to **deadlines**.

4. Pay more attention to **anticipatory scanning techniques**.

5. Make sure you are concentrating on the **key features** of every situation.

6. Take more frequent **rest periods**, even if they are of shorter duration than normal, as these will help to keep you refreshed and alert.

7. Always remember the value of **imaginative and intuitive responses** and the fact that these can occur when you least expect them, perhaps when you are just dropping off to sleep and are really relaxed and stress-free.

8. Seek out the times and places where you know from experience you can maintain good levels of concentration. For many people these are places like libraries, and early mornings or late evenings.

9. Pay attention to the next chapter, which is about speeding up and slowing down appropriately.

10. Check that you have enough of the right kind of activities in your reserve bank.

11. Review your **flexible performance strategies**.

12. Always **analyse your performance critically** along the lines set out in Part 1, Chapter 12.

Chapter Eighteen

MAINTAINING MAXIMUM SPEED

Maintaining maximum speed does not mean going at a task hell for leather without any regard for its difficulty or importance. That is the headless chicken's way.

> *Maintaining maximum speed means operating at the highest speed comfortably possible given all the circumstances, and not being content with anything less than this. It means also facing the inevitable problem of fatigue and overcoming it.*

No matter how fit, young and energetic you may feel yourself, there are bound to be times when you just cannot seem to get done the things you want or have to get done. You feel at the end of the day that you are really no further forward than you were at the beginning of the day. Clearly, something needs to be done about this. There are several possible remedies you can try. It is up to you to refuse to be beaten and to ask yourself how the laidback bear would tackle the problem.

Among the most useful and effective methods are these:

1. Find some way of taking a break, even if only for a short while.

2. Get a change of scene. Try working in a different place with a different environment if you can.

3. Change the activity if you can. Sometimes when you cannot make progress with one thing you can proceed better with another.

4. Tackle the difficult parts of a task first and then, when you are beginning to fade, you will only have the easier parts to worry about.

5. Put some music on if you can. These days you can listen to music through headphones without disturbing someone else who may be working nearby. The music should be the kind you like, but not something that you like so much it becomes more important than the work you are doing.

6. Set a slightly tighter deadline. This may compel better concentration without effort on your part.

7. Review what you did on similar occasions in the past when things did not go as you would have wished. You may identify a long-forgotten method of solving the problem.

8. Consider whether the task really needs doing or not. Sometimes we become embroiled in activities because they seem a good idea at the time, but do not have much relevance for the achievement of our objectives in practice.

9. Discuss with colleagues, if you can, how they overcome fatigue.

10. Avoid using artificial stimulants as these may be addictive. In any case, they simply mask the problem and do not solve it in the long run.

11. Avoid forcing yourself to do something unless it is absolutely vital that, no matter how you feel, the task has to be done.

12. Look through this book to see if a technique suggested for a quite different problem will work for you in this instance. Not everything works for everyone in the way it is supposed to and sometimes unlikely solutions can be the most effective.

Acceleration and Deceleration

When we are driving a car we automatically speed up when the traffic is light and slow down when it becomes heavier. It can be hazardous to our nerves and even our health not to. If we do not speed up when everyone else does we incur the wrath of other drivers. If we do not slow down when the traffic builds up we risk an accident.

Life, however, rarely runs smoothly and we may well encounter situations where it appears impossible to speed up and we may find ourselves in others where the pace of events carries us along willy-nilly. We have to find some way of controlling this kind of situation or we shall find ourselves dashing around frantically again.

Feedback can, of course, tell us whether or not speeding up or slowing down is affecting our performance adversely and we can then react accordingly. That may be one solution.

Effects of Speed on Skill Levels

It is natural to assume that if you increase speed in an activity you will automatically make more mistakes and perform less effectively. This is not necessarily true. If speeds are built up gradually, this gives you time to adjust and become accustomed to the new levels and usually a better performance is the end result.

Responding to Emergencies

Crises will always occur even in completing the best-organised tasks. The immediate reaction of the headless chicken is to panic. This is the least-helpful reaction. **Don't panic** – as Corporal Jones in the TV comedy series *Dads' Army* used to say. Step back and ask why the emergency has arisen. Ask yourself why you did not see it coming, for many emergencies can be predicted. For example, overfill a chip pan and leave it unattended on too high a heat setting and the chances of a chip pan fire are greatly increased.

Where emergencies cannot be predicted, keep a cool head and look for a way out. You would not pour water on a burning chip pan, but cover it quickly with a dampened cloth. This would be both easier and quicker and is the correct laidback-bear approach.

Activity Overloads

Try to do too many things at once and you will very quickly have an emergency on your hands. You have to know your limitations. The headless chicken thinks that he or she can do everything at once. To any sensible person, this is clearly impossible. Set a reasonable target of things to be done within the time available. Resist all attempts by others to force you to go beyond this. I once taught an audiovisual aids technician who was continually overloaded with requests for her skills in producing visual aids for company presentations. She simply could not cope with the demand. I suggested she get a laminated wall planner and put all the requests on it with their deadlines and the names of the senior staff who had requested them. Then, when someone came along with a last-minute request that simply had to be done, she asked them to identify for her the senior member of staff who could be made to wait for their work to be done. Last-minute requests ceased very quickly after that, as no one was prepared to upset superiors and the chart showed them unequivocally just how much pressure her limited time was under. It was not long before she got an assistant as well.

Artificially Induced Urgency

This is simply the kind of haste which does not really need to be there in the first place. It is extremely common among headless chickens and is the result of not allowing sufficient time to complete a task before the deadline, whether that is self-imposed or imposed by others. A common example can be seen in people dashing to get to work in a morning because they are late. This can easily be avoided, of course, by setting off a little earlier. If this means getting out of bed earlier, the loss of sleep can be avoided by going to bed earlier at night. It is a wholly avoidable situation and this is the principal characteristic of urgency which is artificially induced rather than unavoidable.

Chapter Nineteen
EFFECTS OF VARIETY OF ACTIVITY

Variety, they do say, is the spice of life. This is certainly true when it comes to organising a programme of activity for yourself (or someone else, for that matter).

> *Nothing kills drive and initiative and productive working quicker than monotony.*

For this reason, we need to organise our activities in such a way that the amount of time spent on a particular part of an activity is limited. You should have a cut-off point in mind at which you change the activity, if for no other reason than that it will help to solve some of the problems for which possible remedies were suggested in the last chapter. Most people find that about 20 minutes to half an hour on a task is about right if maximum effectiveness is to be maintained. After that time, change to another activity, knowing that you can always return to the previous one when you are ready.

This, of course, is an ideal limit to aim for and in reality longer periods may be necessary, but at least you will be aware that the longer you press ahead with a task the less efficient you become. Variety can help to prevent this fatigue effect from having an adverse effect upon performance.

Discretionary Time
We are all familiar with the 'all work and no play' adage. Many headless chickens become so caught up in their daily activities that they have no time for play. They are always too busy. This is a very

shortsighted approach. You have to examine everything that you feel you have to do and ask yourself, 'Is this really necessary? What will happen if I do not do it?' If the answer is 'Not very much,' you have identified a prime candidate for giving yourself a bit of discretionary time – that is, time which you can use for any purpose you like.

How much discretionary time you need or can provide yourself with will vary from person to person. The average is about 30 hours a week. If you cannot honestly manage as much as this, you have to do the best you can. You will never become a laidback bear otherwise.

Time for thinking and reflection is never time wasted. At the very least it is used for incubation and at best it allows for the creative side of you to have full rein. Many a brilliant idea has been thought of when someone was simply sitting under an apple tree admiring the view, like Newton, or relaxing in the bath, like Archimedes.

In many ways, sitting and thinking, or even just sitting, is the laidback bear's favourite activity. But do not be misled into thinking that somebody who appears to be doing nothing is not involved in a great deal of activity inside their head.

Always remember to build in some discretionary time when you are setting your deadlines.

Deciding Direction
It will help you greatly in your quest to become more of a laidback bear in your approach to tasks if you determine which objectives to pursue first. Basically, you have two choices. You can either tackle the hard task first and leave the easy ones until later, or you can do the easy ones first and then tackle the hard ones later.

The advantage of tackling the easy ones first is that it gives you an easy introduction to your daily work, but means you have to tackle hard tasks when you are beginning to tire and not at your best.

Tackling the hard tasks first means that when you are beginning to tire you are not faced by any really difficult tasks. This is the approach recommended here. Always do the hard things first when you are fresh.

Conflicts Over Time Use

There will always be conflicts over how you are going to use your limited time. Activities will always overlap. After all, life is rarely neat. You will need to make clear decisions over which things can be run in tandem, which will need to be abandoned if there is overlap and which will have to continue and make new tasks wait.

You cannot avoid having to make decisions over time use at all times and you will need to keep your main objectives clearly in mind to help you avoid being unnecessarily sidetracked. Headless chickens are often sidetracked and you will have to make sure that you do not suffer a similar fault.

Changing Perceptions of Time

Perceptions of time change with age, the interest you have in an activity, the time of day and other factors. For this reason, activities need to be timed when you are training yourself to complete them faster without creating undue stress.

The older you are, for instance, the faster time appears to pass. This is probably because any activity is a smaller proportion of the total time you have been on the planet than it is when you are younger.
Interest can cause you to become unaware of the passage of time. You may therefore spend much more time doing something than you originally intended or than you can afford.

Time of day can change your perception. Most people work better in a morning. Some work better in the evening. Almost no one works best in the afternoon. Activities undertaken in the afternoon can therefore appear to drag, even though they may not actually be taking any more time than they would if done in the morning or the evening.

Coping With The Speed and Scale of Change

It is a truism that change is taking place nowadays much faster than it ever has done in the past. If you are to keep up with the increasing speed and scale of change, you have to become extremely adaptable.

You cannot ignore change. That is not an option. You either keep pace with it or you fall behind. The techniques you learn in this book will help you to achieve this and to avoid being relegated to the status of a headless chicken who dashes about looking busy but failing totally to keep in touch with rapidly changing events.

Chapter Twenty

TIMEWASTING

You may be guilty of wasting your own time and if this is the case there should be plenty in this book to help you to avoid the problem in the future. But not all of the causes of wasted time are within your control. Below is a list of causes of wasted time, some of which you can do something about and some of which you cannot. You might like to identify the ones which are the biggest problems for you and see what there is in the rest of this book that will help you to deal effectively with them.

A Timewaster's Checklist

Here is a list of the factors that many people working in organisations have identified as causing them to make inefficient use of their time. Tick the ones that you consider your own timewasters. Make notes on what you intend to do about them:

- ◆ Unclear objectives ❑
- ◆ Inadequate information on which to act ❑
- ◆ Postponed decisions by others ❑
- ◆ Procrastination by you and by others ❑
- ◆ Lack of feedback on whether you have done the right thing ❑
- ◆ Routine work ❑
- ◆ Too much reading ❑
- ◆ Interruptions ❑
- ◆ The telephone ❑
- ◆ No time-planning ❑
- ◆ Meetings ❑
- ◆ Lack of competent personnel to work with ❑
- ◆ Lack of delegation ❑

- ◆ Lack of self-discipline ❑
- ◆ Visitors ❑
- ◆ Training new staff ❑
- ◆ Lack of priorities ❑
- ◆ Unavailability of people ❑
- ◆ Junk mail ❑
- ◆ Outside demands (i.e. any not related to your job) ❑
- ◆ Poor filing system ❑
- ◆ Fatigue ❑
- ◆ Questionnaires ❑
- ◆ Socialising by you and by others involving you ❑
- ◆ Lack of concentration ❑
- ◆ Coffee and tea breaks ❑
- ◆ Unintelligible communications ❑
- ◆ Lack of clerical staff ❑
- ◆ Red tape ❑
- ◆ Pet projects that you spend too much time
  on because you enjoy them ❑
- ◆ Attempting too much at once ❑
- ◆ Span of control (having too many subordinates to supervise) ❑
- ◆ Usurped authority (having your decisions overridden) ❑
- ◆ Can't say 'No' ❑
- ◆ Low morale ❑
- ◆ Mistakes ❑
- ◆ Over-optimism (thinking you can do more than is possible) ❑
- ◆ Employees with problems ❑
- ◆ Failure to listen (by you or by others) ❑
- ◆ Responding to the urgent rather than the important ❑
- ◆ Confused responsibilities ❑
- ◆ Failure to motivate staff ❑
- ◆ Lack of activity or project co-ordination ❑
- ◆ Waiting for decisions ❑
- ◆ Lack of monitoring and review procedures ❑
- ◆ Orientation towards problems rather than opportunities ❑

In your notebook, list any other sources of timewasting that you feel apply to your job.

Part Three:
Application in Personal Skills

This part examines how time creation techniques can be applied to increase speed or save time in the use of personal skills necessary for effective performance at work and in everyday life. It will help headless chickens to further their mastery of laidback-bear approaches.

Chapter Twenty one

THINKING

Although there is considerable controversy about the nature of thinking, one way of defining it is to see it as two kinds of approach to solving problems or to selecting the appropriate course of action to be taken. The two forms thinking takes under this definition are:

1. Convergent, logical, analytical, highly predictable thinking
2. Divergent, creative, insightful, unpredictable thinking.

Headless chickens tend to be poor at the first and not much better at the second, mainly because both kinds of thinking require a certain amount of discipline. Laidback bears take the time to think before acting, and the time they spend doing this is more than saved in avoiding nonproductive activity.

Convergent thinking

This kind of thinking follows logical paths. It looks for a correct answer, converging upon it from the information the thinker has available. It is used to analyse quantifiable problems. Its approaches and often its results are generally predictable.

Convergent thinking is most effective when there is information available which can be handled logically (as in finding the causes of a mechanical breakdown – if your car rolls to a stop on the motorway, you check all the possible causes systematically and logically). It is effective when there is a high probability of there being a single right answer. It is effective in analysing both evidence and arguments.

How well we communicate with each other depends to a large extent on how clearly we think. If our thinking is faulty, then what we say or write will be faulty. At least three kinds of unclear thinking, of which headless chickens tend more often to be afflicted, can be identified.

Emotional thinking

If we base our conclusions about ideas, objects, people, events, and so on, not on the processes of reasoning, but on our emotional reactions to them – whether we like or dislike them, despise or fear them, are pleased or angered by them – we are once again on unsafe ground. Emotional thinking leads to prejudging and prejudice, and as such is unacceptable as a basis for action in a rational, civilised society. It leads to the panicky reaction of the headless chicken.

Dishonest thinking

Here the illogical and emotional processes of thinking are used deliberately to reach conclusions beneficial to an individual and harmful to others. The point about dishonest thinking is that those who use it are shutting their minds to the truth, either consciously because it suits them or unconsciously through lack of self-insight.

Superficial thinking

In this kind of thinking, errors occur and false conclusions are reached simply because the individual has not devoted enough time to thinking about the problem or question. It is the kind of thinking which is particularly encouraged in an age of mass communication, with the preference for the short and the simple – and the trivial. Evidence to support this can be found in the thinking of any headless chicken.

The Characteristics of Clear Thinking

If we are to avoid the faults in thinking discussed above, our thinking should possess at least four main characteristics of which laidback bears are the masterly proponents.

Awareness of the rules of logic

It is easier to say which kinds of thinking break the rules of logic than to state precisely what those rules are but, basically, logical thought is concerned with the relationships between statements rather than with the truth or falsity of particular statements. It is possible to arrive at a logical conclusion which is untrue, if the original statements are untrue. However, the test to prevent this kind of situation arising lies in basing statements on evidence. A logical conclusion, then, is one which follows inescapably from what has been stated previously. An awareness of logic helps us to tell whether faults in our thinking arise from poor information or poor thought processes. It is only when we know the source of any error that we can begin to do something to remedy it.

Avoidance of emotional reactions and prejudices

We can never eliminate entirely the presence of emotion in our reactions to statements, situations, issues or problems, nor can we ever be completely free of prejudice, but, if we can identify the occasions on which we react emotionally and if we can become aware of our own prejudices, we can begin to lessen the influence they have over our thinking. If we are to think clearly, this self-awareness and self-insight are essential, for it simply is not possible for the headless chicken to think rationally and reasonably. Useful discussion should, therefore, be a cool, dispassionate process.

Honesty

We need to be especially honest about our own motives. We may choose to hide those motives from others in order to achieve a specific objective, but we should never be in danger of deluding ourselves about what it is we really want. This self-examination is another essential part of the process of thinking clearly. It also helps considerably, of course, if we can be honest with each other, even over motives. This way we are much more likely to be able to get at the truth of a situation, settle an issue or resolve a problem.

Adequate consideration of problems

This does not refer simply to the need to allow sufficient time for consideration, but refers also to the need for enough evidence on which to base a conclusion. In other words, before we can decide whether the stated relationships between facts, and hence the conclusions drawn from them, are correct, we must first of all check the accuracy of the facts. Thus, we can identify three stages in the process of allowing adequate consideration:

1. Check the accuracy of the information available as thoroughly as possible;
2. Check the validity of the relationships claimed to exist between various pieces of information;
3. Check the logical validity and the truth of the conclusions drawn by reference back to the information from which they stem.

Divergent Thinking

On the other hand, divergent thinking follows few rules. It does not look for a single correct answer, nor indeed necessarily for any answer at all. Starting from a problem, a situation or a set of facts, it diverges, explores, seeks, freewheels, kicks around and examines things from many viewpoints. It is curious, provocative, controversial and even ridiculous. It is used to find new solutions to old problems, new ways of doing things and different approaches to all kinds of situations. It is unpredictable both in method and in results. It is laidback.

It is most effective where logical approaches have failed, or there is insufficient information for them to be used, or their use is inappropriate for any one of a thousand reasons. Divergent thinking is effective when there is a low probability that there is a single right answer or when an unusual, out-of-the-ordinary, insightful interpretation of the facts has to be made to find one, as in devising a name for a new product or re-inventing a corporate identity. It is effective in opening up new fields for exploitation and new areas for development.

Quality of ideas

One of the most difficult problems which faces those new to divergent thinking is that of producing a large enough sample of ideas from which to select one for dealing with the problem. The more that can be generated, the better the chance of finding one that will work.

The importance of deferring judgment

During the time that the ideas are being gathered, nothing should be rejected. Ridiculous ideas, if rejected too soon, will simply make the collection look neat and sensible. But it is also likely to be dull. If ridiculous ideas can be retained for the time being, they may well generate others which offer a sensible but radically new idea, interpretation or approach, so defer judgment during the production of ideas. The time for evaluation comes later. Headless chickens rush to judgment too quickly; laidback bears know to bide their time.

Techniques of Divergent Thinking

Although divergent thinking is, characteristically, unpredictable, there are certain basic principles and approaches which will help to stimulate it. They are of special value to those who are more familiar with the approaches of convergent thinking than with being creative. First of all, the problem must be stated and defined. It should be written down. This is necessary to give thinking a focal point. It will also help to reveal whether or not the subject is one in which divergent thinking can help. For instance, in industry, divergent thinking will be of more use in finding a name for a product or in producing marketing ideas for a product than in deciding whether or not to build a new factory in a particular place.

Secondly, there are at least eight techniques which can be applied to produce creative answers, solutions and suggestions. You should work systematically through the list until a reasonable amount of self-confidence in thinking divergently has been developed. These techniques are as follows:

1. **Generation.** Find as many ways of doing or looking at something as possible. Nothing should be rejected. However unpromising an idea may seem at first, it may acquire significance later.

2. **Challenge the present situation.** Is it really like this? Does it have to be like this? Is there really a problem? Could we look at things in some other way?

3. **Inversion.** Turn things completely round, or upside down. If, for example, a building contractor is designing a new kind of house, he might consider putting the bedrooms downstairs and the living room upstairs. This might in fact be the best way of doing things if the houses are being built on the side of a hill. The service roads could be built level with the upper floors of the houses at the back, and the living rooms would give better views over the surrounding countryside if they were upstairs.

4. **Analogies.** Compare the problem situation or issue to another. They need not be related for this technique to work. For example, comparing roads to railways may give us an idea for small uniform-sized units that could be coupled together and so reduce the traffic in towns while preserving the individuality and the privacy of the car. Again, comparing cars to beads (an unlikely analogy) could lead to the same kind of solution and might even suggest a method of linking car-like units together.

5. **Allow ridiculous ideas.** The motor car, aeroplane and submarine were once ridiculous ideas (not to mention going to the moon).

6. **Waiting for inspiration.** Doing nothing or allowing a period of mental incubation is a useful creative-thinking technique. Once the problem has been stated and defined, the brain will continue to work on it and possible solutions may come to mind at the oddest of times. Solutions discovered in this way can be revolutionary and yet highly practical.

7. **Readiness for insight.** This is closely allied to the previous technique and means being ready 24 hours a day for solutions to present themselves. If they do, they must be noted down straight away. Many good ideas thought of at 1 a.m. have vanished by 8 a.m. if they are not recorded. When illumination comes, one must be ready for it.

8. **Repetition of process.** Going over the same ground again often produces an additional idea which turns out to be the one that will work.

The third step in this approach to creative thinking is to take all ideas, interpretations, insights and solutions that have been produced and evaluate them. The process of evaluation is best carried out after at least an overnight break. The aim should be to try to identify the idea or solution which is most likely to succeed and which therefore is the one to be tried first.

Questioning

Many people are prevented from thinking divergently because they are quite content to accept things as they are. Even if they seek change, they look for improvements based on keeping things pretty much as they are. Change, in these circumstances, becomes minimal and to all intents and purposes the problems remain.

You should acquire the habit of questioning everything. Why is it like this? Why do we do it this way? 'Why?' is the most creative question you can ask, because it is the necessary first step to seeking new ideas.

Unless you challenge what is, you will never know what could be.

Facility in doing this can be increased in much the same way as quantities of ideas are collected. A question is posed and then, within a time limit, all the solutions offered are taped or noted down.

Individual Brainstorming

Brainstorming sessions are usually group affairs, with everyone sitting around throwing ideas into a common 'pool' for later evaluation. The evidence that is available, however, indicates that more (and better) ideas are produced when people work individually on a topic than when they work as a group. The procedure to use, then, is as follows:

1. The problem to be the subject for brainstorming should be selected.
2. You should write your ideas down as quickly as you can without stopping to analyse their practicality.
3. It helps if 10 minutes is devoted to a warm-up session. Write down as many solutions to a specimen problem as you can think of in the time. See exercise 2 on page 42.
4. The main subject for brainstorming should then be written down.
5. The brainstorming session proper should follow and should last for about 30 minutes. The eight techniques described above may be used at any time that you wish.
6. You should write down as many solutions to the problem as you can think of in the time. No solution should be censored or rejected at this stage.
7. At the end of the brainstorming session, put your list away for 24 hours before trying to evaluate it. Headless chickens find it hard to do this, but it is necessary if you are to avoid rejecting fresh and unusual solutions.

Uses and value of divergent thinking

Most participants will by now have realised that divergent thinking techniques are of most use in finding new things to do, new ways of doing things, new interpretations and new outlooks. They are indeed invaluable not only in promoting change and development, but also in indicating precisely where and in which ways change and development can take place.

Chapter Twenty Two
READING

Eye Movements in Reading

If you move your head slowly from side to side when your eyes are focused on a stationary object, your eyes will appear to move smoothly in their sockets. If, on the other hand, you keep your head still and move your eyes slowly from side to side, your eyes will move in a series of jerks (or 'saccades'). The pauses between movements are called fixations. When reading, the eyes move in a series of saccades, with brief fixations (0.25 to 0.35 of a second) between movements. The eye can only accept information, it is now believed, when stationary and, in fact, a mechanism in the brain switches vision off while the eyes are in motion. Even in the first kind of eye movement described above, where the eye is focused on an object, eye movements are still saccadic, but the movements and the consequent fixations are so small and so rapid that the eyes do appear to move smoothly.

The amount of information taken in at each fixation depends on the reader's span of perception (or eye span). The quickness with which the eyes can enable perception of one piece of information (a word or group of words) and move on to the next depends on speed of perception (fixation time can be reduced to 0.1 of a second and speeds of 0.001 are possible in certain circumstances).

Indeed, since poor eye movements are merely a symptom and not a cause of poor reading, there would be little to be achieved simply by making the eyes move in a certain way. But, if by the end of working through the ideas described in this chapter, reading performance has improved, then it is reasonable to infer that both speed and span of perception have been increased. One cannot happen without the other.

The approach here, however, will be to allow the physiological improvement in eye movements to arise naturally out of a preoccupation with comprehending the written word faster and better. For reading is concerned with understanding meaning, and actual technique is a secondary consideration. If reading matter could be understood by holding it up to the ear, then this would be a valid reading technique. Conversely, if there is no comprehension then a technique cannot be called a reading technique, even if every word on a page has been looked at several times.

Reading is comprehension or it is nothing.

The terms 'reading speed' and 'comprehension', as used here and elsewhere, refer respectively to speed of comprehension and quality of comprehension in reading. The fact that the two are simply parts of the same process, rather than separate entities, should not be forgotten.

Differences between Poor and Good Readers

The most important differences between poor and good readers are as follows:

Poor reader	Good reader
Physiological differences	
1. Has narrow eye span.	Has wider eye span.
2. Has lower speed of perception.	Has a higher speed of perception.
3. Lacks rhythm in reading.	Has rhythmic, confident eye movements.
4. Tends to read slowly all the time.	Is a flexible reader who reads everything as quickly as purposes in reading and the nature of the material will allow.

Poor reader	Good reader
5. Regresses (goes back to read things again) habitually.	Avoids all unnecessary regressions.
6. Vocalises (cannot read silently) or subvocalises (suffers from 'inner speech' or 'reading aloud silently').	Does not vocalise and reduces subvocalisation by reading faster.

Psychological differences

Poor reader	Good reader
7. Is unsure about purposes in reading.	Always has a clear knowledge of purposes and expectations before reading.
8. Is tense when reading under pressure (e.g. lack of time).	Remains relaxed even when reading 'against the clock'.
9. Is not able to anticipate the nature of subsequent material when reading.	Anticipates well the general nature of material yet to be read when reading.
10. Lacks concentration except for short periods.	Concentrates well by avoidance or exclusion of distractions.
11. Is unable to retain information for very long after reading.	Has good retention of information over longer periods.

Educational differences

Poor reader	Good reader
12. Has a limited vocabulary.	Extends vocabulary by wide reading.
13. Is unable to read critically.	Always reads critically, even at speed.
14. Has a limited general background of knowledge and experience.	Has a wide general background of knowledge and experience and a thoughtful and critical approach to both.

You should aim to be able to place yourself in the right-hand column on as many of these points as possible. The first two differences have already been dealt with, but let us look briefly at some of the others. More rhythmic eye movements will develop with increased speed, so we do not need to take any particular action on this point. Flexibility will develop as a result of practising the approaches outlined in this chapter.

Regression can be prevented by either a simple act of will or by drawing a postcard down over material as it is read. If regression is a problem, the best cure is to eliminate it altogether, at least during practice. Comprehension will suffer a little at first, but will soon recover. Evidence suggests that regressions add no more than 3–7 per cent to your comprehension level, so in most cases no great loss will be experienced by eliminating them.

Subvocalisation need not hinder increases in speed. It has been found that people can read aloud at speeds up to nearly 300 words per minute (wpm), so where the 'reading aloud' does not actually go as far as involving the vocal cords, higher speeds than this should be possible. Since the primary form of language is speech and not writing, it is inevitable that many readers should subvocalise.

Subvocalisation can also be a powerful aid to comprehension, so, having noted its existence, we won't regard it as a problem and will forget about it. Higher speeds in any case tend to make its presence less pronounced, though it may never disappear altogether, even when skimming (a range of techniques described later).

What is Comprehension?

The point has already been made that 'reading speed' and 'comprehension' are not two separate activities, but merely two parts of the same process – that of understanding the meaning and significance of the printed word. Comprehension is, of course, a general skill that we use on all the information that is communicated to us by whatever means and through whichever of our senses. It is worth mentioning, therefore, that, although we are here concerned with comprehension when reading, any improvement in speed or quality achieved will be reflected in other uses of comprehension skills. Similarly, improvements effected generally will result in better reading.

Many readers assume that there is an inverse relationship between reading speed and comprehension, and that if speed is increased then comprehension will automatically fall. If this were so, there would be little point in a chapter such as this one. Fortunately it is not and, in fact, the average reader can increase his or her reading speed by about 80 per cent without loss of comprehension.

Comprehension comprises a number of abilities. Chief among these are the abilities:

1. to recall information from the material;

2. to select important points and draw general conclusions;

3. to make deductions from what has been read, draw inferences, be aware of implications and carry out other interpretative activities;

4. to relate what has been read to prior knowledge and experience and to use this in achieving a better and deeper understanding of the material;

5. to use all the other activities mentioned above to evaluate the material and discuss it intelligently.

It should also be possible for you to test these abilities for yourself on materials that you encounter during the course of a normal reading week.

How can Comprehension be Improved?

Quality of comprehension is affected by speed – beyond certain limits. We have already said that higher speeds do not automatically mean lower comprehension scores. It is true, however, that if you read too quickly at any point in your progress to higher speeds then comprehension will suffer. Speed increases need to be achieved gradually to prevent this happening.

Other factors which affect comprehension include:

1. the reasons or purposes for which the material is being read;

2. your motivation for, or interest in, reading the material;

3. the nature, content and level of difficulty of the material;

4. the layout of the material;

5. the environment in which the reading is being done.

The quality of your comprehension can be improved by making sure that each of the above factors is taken into consideration. The three main ways, however, of improving comprehension are as follows:

1. by testing: (i) retention of information;
   (ii) interpretation of information.

2. by discussion.

3. by wide, varied reading.

You should take steps to make sure that the reading you do in the course of a week or a month contains sufficient breadth and mixture of materials to provide your comprehension skills with the challenge and variety needed to improve them.

Comprehension can also be improved by getting into the habit of approaching all written material critically. Critically means not simply looking for faults and defects, but also looking for points of merit so that reasonably accurate judgments and evaluations may be made about the material. A systematic approach to critical reading has the acronymic title **CITE** (we encountered a form of it in Part 1 Chapter 12) and the procedures involved are quite simple.

As you read and after you have read something, consider the following:

1. **Content.** Ask questions like:
   - What does the material tell me?
   - Is the information accurate or plausible?
   - What is the writer's authority or reliability?

2. **Intentions.** Ask questions like:
   ◆ What is the writer trying to achieve?
   ◆ Who is the material aimed at?

3. **Treatment.** Ask questions like:
   ◆ Am I being convinced by reason or emotion?
   ◆ Is there any evidence of bias?
   ◆ Has the treatment influenced my opinion unduly?

4. **Evaluation.** Ask questions like:
   ◆ If the writer fails, how, where and why does he or she fail?
   ◆ In the light of the answers to these questions, what is my evaluation of the material?

Defining Purposes and Expectations in Reading

Speeds in reading and, indeed, your whole approach to reading matter, should be determined by:

1. purposes and expectations in reading;

2. the nature of the material.

You should aim always to read as quickly as these two factors will allow.

On each piece of reading material a range of speeds will be possible. For the average reader the range will be narrow, probably extending from 150 wpm to no higher than 300 wpm. For the efficient reader the range may extend up to 800 wpm. The aim should therefore be always to achieve a speed as close as possible to the upper limit on each piece of reading matter. It is easy to be content with a lower speed but the efficient reader will be conscious of the fact that time can be saved without sacrifice in quality and that this will guard against unnecessary slackness in approach.

In order to achieve the degree of efficiency implied by this approach, it is important to define purposes and expectations in reading as clearly as possible. It is important to go beyond primary or obvious purposes and it should be possible to identify with reasonable ease three levels of purpose, as follows:

Primary	Secondary (examples)	Tertiary (examples)
Have to read.	Solve a problem. Increase special knowledge. Make a decision.	Acquire relevant facts. Acquire new facts. Acquire unusual facts.
Want to read.	Derive pleasure. Self-education. Evaluate critically.	Acquire interesting facts. Acquire important facts. Acquire insight into facts.

Not all the possible purposes have been given in the above illustration and you will be able to add many secondary and tertiary purposes of your own.

You should know the reasons why you are reading as specifically and as clearly as possible before you begin reading.

Also, before you read something, you will have certain expectations about the material. You may know the kind of information it is likely to contain or you may know that the writer will be trying to persuade you to accept a particular point of view.

You should be consciously aware of your expectations before you decide how to read the material.

Assessing materials

In addition to defining purposes and expectations as clearly as possible, you should make a brief assessment of the material before reading it. This can be done during a quick preview (or skimming) of the material to obtain an overview, or general impression, which covers the following points:

1. the writer's purposes in writing;
2. the length of the material;
3. the level of difficulty of the material;
4. the reliability of the material, perhaps through information given about the writer;
5. the nature of the content of the material, in terms of the pattern of organisation, the subject matter and the importance and/or relevance of the content.

This preview need take no more than a few seconds and it should concentrate on identifying the pattern of organisation which the writer has imposed upon the material. This will help both in deciding how much time and attention to give to it and in assimilating the information if it is decided that the material should, in fact, be read at all.

Patterns of Organisation of Written Material

If the same set of facts is given to 10 different writers, they will produce 10 different pieces of writing, some of which may differ so much as to make it unclear that they are all concerned with the same subject. The most obvious difference will be in the words that each writer chooses to express what he or she wants to say. You should therefore try to 'see through' the words used to the information, the facts, ideas or feelings that the writer wants you to understand.

Your concern is with assimilating meaning rather than the word sequence which communicates that meaning. There are certain exceptions to this rule, but it holds broadly true.

This process is helped if you can identify the pattern of organisation a writer has used. Once the general outline has been perceived, a number of other things are made easier.

An awareness of the pattern of organisation which the writer has imposed on his or her material helps:

◆ in defining purposes more closely

◆ in making a more accurate choice of reading techniques

◆ in anticipating while reading

◆ in relating specific information to its context in the general framework.

The pattern of organisation can be looked at in three distinct ways, according to:

1. the type of writing;

2. the structural principles which all written materials follow;

3. the patterns peculiar to specific kinds of material.

Types of writing

There are four types of writing:

◆ description

◆ exposition

◆ argument

◆ narrative.

Where the types are mixed, one will dominate. If the principal type can be identified, an approach can be chosen to suit it.

In **description**, you will concentrate on building up the mental picture that the writer wishes you to see. In **exposition**, you will be looking for a logical ordering of points, for stages of development and for facts. In **argument**, you will be looking for 'pros' and 'cons', for evidence and reasons, and for the outline of the case that is being made. In **narrative**, you will be looking for chronological development and for movement from one place to another.

Structure of written materials

When it comes to using the principles of structure to help you, it is far more useful to regard the paragraph as a unit of meaning than the sentence. Often in a paragraph one sentence will contain the essential information that the rest of the paragraph seeks to expand on. If a writer has something important to say, it makes sense to place it in a position of natural emphasis. In a paragraph, there are two such positions: one at the beginning and one at the end. And the beginning of the paragraph carries greater emphasis than the end, so more key sentences will be placed first in paragraphs than in any other position. You should examine one of the sections in this chapter that you have already read and confirm that this is so. An efficient reader will move quickly from paragraph to paragraph, picking up the main idea or fact in each one and relating subordinate facts and ideas to it, and then moving quickly on again.

Patterns of specific materials

The use that can be made of an awareness of patterns peculiar to specific kinds of material will be discussed in greater detail later. But with articles, for example, the thesis is usually stated in the opening few paragraphs, there are limited numbers of points being made and there is often a re-statement in the closing paragraphs. In newspapers the use of headings and subheadings can guide or mislead and care needs to be taken. There is a variety of short items together with longer articles. News articles, for example, will often be written so that they can be cut from the end forwards without much loss when new stories come in. Reports in industry will have clearly defined sections – summary, conclusions, introduction, the body of the report and appendixes. All of this information can assist you in knowing where to look for what kind of information and in assimilating it once found.

Level of difficulty of written material

It will also help if you are aware of the factors which can affect the level of difficulty of written material. Easy material can clearly be handled much more rapidly than difficult material and you need to know the level of difficulty of the material you are dealing with so that you can change your technique to suit it. Some of the main factors which can affect level of difficulty are:

1. **The vocabulary range of the material.** The broader it is or the more specialised, the more difficult it will be to read the material.

2. **The subject of the material.** Some subjects are inherently more difficult than others, especially 'abstract' subjects like philosophy.

3. **The interest value of the material.** Some subjects are inherently more interesting than others, especially those with strong 'human interest'.

4. **The writer's competence in using language.** Abstruseness can make life very difficult for the reader.

5. **The layout of the material and the way it is printed.** The type must be of a reasonable size and lines should be neither too short nor too long.

6. **The environment in which the reading is being done.** If there is too much noise or other distractions, reading can become very difficult.

Flexibility

Not every piece of writing is of equal importance and the aim should be to conserve energy for material that is more demanding.

Flexibility is the key to efficiency in reading.

To encourage flexibility, you should ask the following questions:

1. Am I spending enough (or too much) time reading this material?

2. Am I taking enough (or too much) care over my reading on this occasion?

3. Am I making enough (or too much) effort to understand what I am reading?

Most of us are taught at school that the only way to read well is to read slowly. But we can clearly read the *Daily Mirror* well at a higher speed than we need to use to read *The Guardian* well. We can read a leaflet intended for the general public faster than we can read a Government White Paper. There are many kinds of material which do not justify close attention and there are many occasions on which we do not have time for a leisurely approach. We must learn to use our 'gears'.

'Gears' in Reading Speeds

There are four 'gears' in reading speeds and each has its own characteristics.

Gear	Speed range (approx)	Characteristics
1. Studying.	0-200 wpm	Reading, re-reading, making notes, revising.
2. Slow reading.	150-300 wpm	Word-by-word, line-by-line progress, often with regressions.
3. Rapid reading.	300-800 wpm	Wordgroup-by-wordgroup, line-by-line, regression-free progress.
4. Skimming.	600-60,000 w.p.m.	Allowing the eyes to break away from line-by-line progress and move rapidly across and down the page.

It might be wise to remind you at this point that 'words per minute' is merely a measure of speed, like 'kilometres per hour' and 60,000 wpm for the upper limit of skimming does not mean that so many words have been assimilated in the space of a single minute. This is, in fact, the kind of speed that is achieved when the pages of a book are turned over one at a time as quickly as is physically possible. Nonetheless, more information can be obtained about a book by doing this than simply by looking at the table of contents. It is a useful technique for a quick preview.

Use of 'gears'

You will be able to devise uses for the various 'gears' that suit your own needs and requirements, but a guide may be helpful.

Purpose	Material	Suggested Technique
Outline only	Easy	Skimming
	Average	Skimming
	Difficult	Rapid reading
General understanding	Easy	Skimming
	Average	Rapid reading
	Difficult	Slow reading
Detailed understanding	Easy	Rapid reading
	Average	Slow reading
	Difficult	Studying

Systematic reading

The flexibility that you should now be concentrating on developing needs to be built into a systematic approach if it is to produce the best results and make you a laidback-bear reader. One approach, which has been used successfully by a large number of readers who have attended the reading-improvement courses I have given, has the mnemonic title **PACER**. It operates as a series of steps which the reader takes in dealing with reading matter. Not everything will pass through all five steps. Much will be rejected after the first one and other material will have been adequately dealt with by the end of the fourth step. A minority of the material encountered will be subjected to all five steps. The system thus has a built-in flexibility, in addition to permitting the fullest use of the four reading 'gears'.

Briefly, the steps of the method are as follows:

1. **P**review everything before reading it. If the material must be read, proceed to the second step.

2. **A**ssess your purposes in going on to read the material and your expectations of what the writer wishes to communicate to you. It is possible, of course, that these will be known in advance or will be discovered during the preview. The purpose in putting this step here is to make sure that it has been done, for the next step cannot be taken without it.

3. **C**hoose the most appropriate reading 'gear' or technique (or combination of techniques).

4. **E**xpedite handling of the material by reading it as decided, but be flexible and change 'gear' if necessary. If the material is important, proceed to the next step.

5. **R**eview what has been read to check that comprehension is adequate for the original purposes in reading the material.

This systematic approach will suit many readers, but those who wish to design their own systems should not be deterred from doing so. The only real requirements are that the approach should be systematic and produce good results, and not leave you frantically shuffling papers like a headless chicken.

Skimming

Skimming should not be confused with reading, but it is a valid and useful reading technique.

Skimming involves allowing the eyes to break away from line-by-line movements and move quickly across and down the page.

There are three main types of skimming:

1. Sampling (600+ wpm). This is skimming the easy, or lazy way, simply by reading selectively. If there is close attention to the opening sentences of paragraphs as well as to any headings or sub-headings, a good level of comprehension can be maintained.

The principle is simply to move on to the next paragraph as soon as the meaning of one can be perceived. Sometimes it may be necessary to go back, but not often. The less of the material that is read, the higher the speed will be. A good overview should be possible with this method, with practice.

2. Previewing (1,000 w.p.m.). This is a combination of selective reading and locating techniques. The eyes should be actively looking for information that will satisfy your purposes in reading as well as paying attention to headings, subheadings and the opening and closing sentences of paragraphs. This type of skimming demands a clearer definition of purposes, better concentration and better anticipation skills but it can be used effectively, with practice. It can be a useful substitute when there is not time to read a particular piece of reading matter in full.

3. Locating (2,000+ w.p.m.). This is the kind of technique that we all habitually use when handling telephone and other directories, dictionaries and handbooks. It demands the clearest possible definition or purpose for effectiveness. Given this, its use can be extended to other kinds of reading. The higher the speed, the further apart the fixation points. The highest speed attainable is about 60,000 w.p.m. or as fast as the pages of a book can be turned over. These very high speeds can, with practice, provide a surprising amount of information, especially for choosing between books to read.

Purposes and uses of skimming

Some examples of the uses of different types of skimming are as follows:

Sampling

1. As a substitute for reading when time is short.

2. To assess the level of difficulty of material.

3. To decide whether to read and to help in the selection of material.

4. To obtain overview and pattern or organisation.

Previewing

1. As a substitute for reading when time is short.

2. To obtain overview and pattern of organisation.

3. As a means of defining purposes in reading.

4. To supplement other reading techniques in systematic reading.

5. To assess the relevance of material to your immediate needs.

Locating

1. To decide whether to read and to help in selection of material.

2. To locate specific information.

3. In using dictionaries, directories and handbooks.

4. In reading classified advertisements in newspapers.

Perhaps the two main uses of skimming are:
1. *as a substitute for reading when time is short.*
2. *to obtain an overview of material before reading.*

Combination with other techniques

PACER has already been described, but a really simple combination that has been found to satisfy a large number of reading requirements is that of previewing and rapid reading. Usually the previewing enables material to be read at a significantly higher speed than would otherwise be the case because of the overview provided by it. Laidback bears know that it takes the stress out of faster and more efficient reading.

Chapter Twenty Three

WRITING

This chapter does not offer a comprehensive course in the principles and techniques of effective writing. Instead, it seeks to deal only with those which are basic to the essential writing needs of those headless chickens who wish to become laidback bears. Nor does it contain much grammatical or other 'technical' information about language. It aims to increase effectiveness in writing by providing guidance in the use of language and by offering opportunities for the practice of basic principles and techniques. This should do more to help avoid the pointless panic of the headless chickens and replace it with the calm, considered approach of the laidback bears.

Poor and Good Writers Compared

The most important differences between poor (headless chickens) and good (laidback bears) writers are as follows:

Poor writer	Good writer
1. Does not always check the accuracy of what is written	Makes sure that what is written is accurate (i.e., that the facts are correct and the content is reliable).
2. Does not control the length of what is written.	Writes as briefly and concisely as the subject matter will allow.
3. Meaning is not always clear.	Makes sure that readers will clearly understand what is written.
4. Pays little attention to keeping writing as simple as possible.	Keeps what is written as simple as the complexity of the content will allow.

Poor writer	Good writer
5. Is unable to suit the order and arrangement of what he or she has to say to purposes in writing and the nature of the material to ensure effectiveness.	Writes effectively by suiting the order and arrangement of what he or she has to say to purposes in writing and the nature of the material itself.
6. Has no clear sense of purpose in writing.	Defines purposes clearly before writing.
7. Carries out preparatory work haphazardly and does not write to a plan.	Prepares and plans writing systematically.
8. Is unable to change style of writing to suit different purposes or materials.	Has the flexibility to change style of writing to suit different purposes and materials.
9. Writing contains many common structural and grammatical errors.	Writes correctly, within the limits allowed by currently acceptable usage.
10. Writes only when it cannot be avoided.	Enjoys writing and takes pride in it.
11. Has a limited vocabulary.	Has a wide and constantly developing vocabulary.
12. Has difficulty in spelling correctly.	Spells correctly.
13. Has difficulty in punctuating writing effectively.	Uses appropriate punctuation with ease and effectiveness.
14. Writing has no identifiable style and is not easy to read rapidly and efficiently.	Has a clearly identifiable personal writing style, which can be read rapidly and efficiently.
15. Writes illegibly.	Writes legibly.

Poor writer	Good writer
16. Has a limited general background of knowledge.	Has a broad general background of knowledge and experience and a thoughtful and critical approach to both.

Accuracy

The laidback writer must check that whatever he or she writes is accurate. That is to say, the facts should be verifiable, the arguments should be soundly based, the reasoning should be logical, and so on. Nothing should be written down which will misinform, mislead or unfairly persuade a reader. This is particularly true both in academic and industrial writing.

Accurate information is an essential basis for effective communication.

Brevity

Nothing that is written down should be longer than it need be. But brevity should not be achieved at the expense of omitting essential and significant information. The test to apply in achieving this is not 'Can it be left out?' but 'Must it go in?' Laidback bears never like doing unnecessary work.

Clarity

It is a relatively simple matter for writers to make things clear to their own satisfaction, but they must also make an effort to ensure that readers will understand them as clearly. One way to achieve this is to allow a period of at least 24 hours to elapse between the first draft of material and its revision. This should permit writers to approach the material with a degree of objectivity and ask themselves whether their readers will understand them readily.

Simplicity

It will usually happen that if material is accurate, brief and clear, it will also be as simple as it is possible to make it without distorting the meaning. It is also possible that if a writer can reduce what he or she wishes to communicate to its essentials, this will help to see whether it is accurate, brief and clear or not.

> *Remember the KISS principle: Keep It Short and Simple.*

Many of the difficulties that are experienced in communication can be traced to unnecessary complexity in expression. The reason is probably that too many writers overestimate the reading abilities of the people for whom the material is intended. The average reader has a reading speed of about 225 wpm and a comprehension level of no more than 75 per cent for most of the materials they are likely to read in the course of a normal week. They are therefore not capable of tackling things of any great difficulty, especially if they have a limited amount of time available for reading.

Effectiveness
This will emerge from the general effect of a writer's attention to the specific considerations, such as those discussed above, but the key to effectiveness probably lies in suiting the order and arrangement of what is being communicated to the purposes in writing and to the nature of the material itself. There are basically three ways in which points can be ordered. These are:

1. Chronological order..
2. The order of ascending importance, in which the main point comes last.
3. The order of descending importance, in which the main point comes first.

Before writers begin to plan their material, they should decide which of these arrangements will best meet their requirements. If the material is long, it is quite possible that all three arrangements will be used in different parts.

Purposes in Writing

We have already stressed the importance of defining purposes as clearly as possible before communicating. The point has to be made again here, for unless you know why you are writing – that is, what you hope to achieve by writing – you cannot write effectively. In defining your purposes you need to know:

1. The subject you have to write about;

2. The form the writing has to take (report, letter, memo etc.);

3. Who will read the material;

4. The result it is hoped the material will achieve.

You should preferably write this information down, together with any other reasons you have for writing, so that you can refer to it as the need arises when you are writing.

At this point an incubation period of the kind described in Part 1 Chapter 6 should be inserted into the process if at all possible. This will help in performing the tasks involved in the next stage.

Planning

The preparatory work for a piece of writing and the writing itself should be carefully planned. A few people have the ability to write well without forethought, but most of us find that planning helps to make the difficult task of writing a little easier. The main sections of the plan can be lettered (a), (b), (c), etc. and the points to be included in each section should be numbered (i), (ii), (iii), etc., even though these headings may not appear in the final draft (especially, for example, in the case of an article, a letter or an essay).

Collection of information
Whatever the writing task, one pitfall to avoid is the too early selection of information to be presented. The writer's first task is to collect. On most occasions, it is desirable to collect a good deal more

information than will actually be used. This enables some useful distillation to take place so that the final draft contains only relevant and necessary information.

Selection of information

The two questions to ask in selecting the information to go into a piece of writing are:

1. Is it relevant to the subject?

2. Is it necessary to include it?

If positive answers cannot be provided to both questions, the information should be omitted.

Arrangement of information

If the preparatory work has been carefully planned, this will make the arrangement of the selected information much easier.

The main point that you have to watch is that the chosen arrangement should be both logical and suited to the purpose in writing. It will usually follow the same pattern as that chosen for the preparatory planning, with any amendments made necessary by, for example, an inability to collect certain information or by the need to be more strictly selective because of considerations of time or space.

Writing

Once the information to be presented has progressed through the stages of collection, selection and arrangement, you now come to what most people regard as the most difficult stage of all, the actual writing. However, if the earlier stages have been given proper attention, writing becomes a much easier (and even pleasurable) activity. At this point, another incubation period of the kind described in Part 1 Chapter 6 should be inserted into the process if at all possible. This will help in performing the tasks involved in this stage. Laidback bears are very fond of incubation periods because they produce results without effort.

As a general rule, each point in the arrangement plan or outline will require a separate paragraph. If paragraphs are too long, however, it is desirable to find some means by which they can be condensed or split into two or more paragraphs.

Shorter paragraphs make for easier and faster reading. Usually, each paragraph will contain one sentence which expresses the main point the paragraph is seeking to develop. It is helpful to a reader if this 'key' or 'topic' sentence can be placed at the beginning of the paragraph.

Since the beginning of a paragraph has a certain natural emphasis, this approach will also help you to give proper weight to your important points.

If main points cannot, for stylistic or other reasons, be stated first, the position which has the second greatest amount of natural emphasis is at the end of the paragraph. Important statements which are tucked away deep in the heart of paragraphs may be undervalued or missed altogether by many readers.

The construction of the sentences which go to make up a paragraph should be as varied as possible.

The basic sentence pattern is one in which, for example, the subject is stated first, then what the subject is doing and lastly who or what the subject is doing it to (i.e., the object). This can easily become monotonous and usually it is possible to make the same point in a number of ways. An example will make some of the possibilities apparent.

Basic pattern

◆ The headless chicken switched on the machine without checking it first and received an electric shock.

Alternative patterns

◆ Because it did not first check the machine, the headless chicken received an electric shock when it switched it on.

◆ By switching its machine on without checking it first, the headless chicken received an electric shock.

◆ Having switched its machine on without checking it first, the headless chicken received an electric shock.

◆ The headless chicken received an electric shock because it had switched its machine on without checking it first.

How many more ways of writing down the above sentence can you find?

Types of Writing

There are four main categories into which most kinds of written materials can be placed. In many materials, more than one type will be present but one will usually dominate the others and set the general tone and style. The principal characteristics of the four types of writing are as follows.

Description

The writer is using words to create a mental picture for the reader. The key words and phrases will be those which describe colour, shape, size, length, appearance and other qualities. Particular attention should be paid to choosing those which most accurately and appropriately give a reader the information necessary to be able to build up the picture in his mind's eye.

Exposition

Here the aim will be to explain how something works, to give the facts about a situation, or to make an objective and accurate statement of some kind. Particular attention should be paid to organising the material so that it offers a logical progression from stage to stage. Care must be taken that nothing is omitted that the reader will need in order to understand the relationship of one part of the material to another.

Argument

Points supporting an argument should be clearly distinguished from those against. Evidence and reasons should be stated clearly and concisely, and facts distinguished from opinions. If a reader is to be persuaded to agree with your case, the best course is to be as honest as possible with him and to avoid attempts to mislead by concealing information which does not support the case or by using dishonest tricks of argument.

Narrative

Here the writer takes the reader through time and place in order to tell a fictional or factual story. Care needs to be taken that no significant event is overlooked and that minor matters are not given more weight than they deserve and so confuse a reader. Too much detail in a narrative can quickly obscure the essential progress of the story.

Readability

At no time should the search for a style cloud a writer's essential desire to make life as easy and pleasant as possible for readers. In recent years a number of formulas have been devised to enable a writer to gauge how difficult a reader will find material. Some of these readability or 'fog' indexes are themselves complex and difficult to calculate, but a simplified method will give a reasonably reliable indication of readability. There are five simple steps to carry out.

1. Select three passages of 100 words each from the material to be assessed.
2. Count the number of sentences in each sample of 100 words. Do not count any part sentence as a sentence, unless it contains more than 10 words. Divide 100 by the number of sentences to obtain the average length.

3. Count the number of words which contain more than two syllables each. Count each long word each time it occurs if it appears more than once. This gives the percentage of hard words in the passage.

4. Add the average sentence length to the percentage of hard words. Multiply by 0.4. Do this for each sample.

5. Add the three figures together and divide by three to obtain an average. The higher the resulting figure, the more difficult the material. A figure higher than 12 indicates difficulty in the material. The lower the figure a writer can obtain by shortening his sentences and reducing the number of long words, the better he will please his readers.

The readability level of this section, for instance, is 9.1.

Practical hints to increase readability

1. **Omit unnecessary words from sentences.**
   ◆ The courage and bravery of the bear was admired and praised by the chickens.
   ◆ The courage of the bear was praised by the chickens.

2. **Use the active statement form wherever possible.**
   ◆ The courage of the bear was praised by the chickens. (Passive)
   ◆ The chickens praised the courage of the bear. (Active)

3. **Omit qualifying phrases unless they are essential to the sense of sentences.**
   ◆ The chickens, somewhat enthusiastically in the circumstances, praised highly the courage of the bear.
   ◆ The chickens praised highly the courage of the bear.

4. **Keep sentences as short as possible.**
   ◆ The chickens, who had never had to fight their opponents so fiercely before, praised the courage of the bear.
   ◆ The chickens praised the courage of the bear. They had never had to fight so fiercely before.

5. **Change long words and phrases to shorter ones where possible.**
   - The feathered avians expressed their approbation of the intrepidity of their quadruped adversary.
   - The chickens praised the courage of the bear.

6. **Make sure you know the exact meanings of the words you use** and use them in appropriate contexts.
   - The chickens exalted the courage of the bear.
   - The chickens praised (or extolled) the courage of the bear.

7. **Preserve the unity of each sentence and each paragraph.** In other words, each sentence should have one subject and each paragraph should deal with a single topic.
   - The chickens praised the courage and their cockerels admired the battle strategy of the bear.
   - The chickens praised the courage of the bear. Their cockerels admired its battle strategy.

8. **Keep the reader in mind all the time when you are writing** and try to write in such a way that he or she will understand. Ask yourself: Will this be clear to someone else?

Presentation and layout

The way a piece of writing looks on the page can be nearly as important as what it contains. If material looks unattractive, it will not be read except by those who have to read it. Even then, it will not make so great an impact as it will if it is carefully set out and attractively presented.

Generally speaking:

- The more space that can be allowed the better

- Handwritten material must be clearly legible

- Margins should be generous

- Spacing between paragraphs and sections of the material should be similarly unstinting.

Headings, where used, should be clear and helpful to the reader. There are many occasions, for instance in certain kinds of reports, when lettering or numbering headings can be additionally helpful.

Final Analysis of Written Materials

Before it is regarded as being finally finished, a piece of writing should be checked carefully. The following questions indicate some of the points to be considered in doing this:

1. Are there any unnecessary repetitions?
2. Is each part of the whole complete in itself?
3. Is each part in the right place?
4. Is any part irrelevant or in need of rewriting?
5. Have any important details been overlooked?
6. Is there any ambiguity?
7. Has the reader been kept in mind all the time?
8. Is the whole arrangement of the material exactly suited to the purpose in writing?
9. Does the material read smoothly?
10. Is it a complete and well-ordered whole?

Chapter Twenty four

LISTENING AND SPEAKING

We now turn our attention to information exchanged by means of the spoken word. Let us first of all, however, look at the nature of listening skills and consider how they may be improved and help in the transformation from headless chicken to laidback bear.

The Nature of Listening Skills

Of all the communication skills, none has been more neglected than listening. There is almost no training in listening provided in our schools and colleges. Such little training as does occur takes place incidentally during training in oral expression. Yet our ability in aural comprehension probably provides us with the basis of most of our knowledge and awareness of the people and the world around us. Headless chickens never listen. They are too busy keeping busy.

Differences between hearing and listening

As the terms are used in this chapter, 'hearing' is a passive, random accidental activity and 'listening' is active, purposeful and systematic.

> *We hear all the sounds that there are to be heard, waking or sleeping; we listen to the particular sounds which either catch our attention or are communicating something we want to know.*

All those of us who are not actually deaf can hear; very few of us have developed the essential skills of listening that we increasingly need in a world in which the spoken word is rapidly becoming more important than the written. If we do not develop our listening skills, we fail to operate with full effectiveness as students, workers, managers, citizens or anything else.

The importance of the ability to listen

Without efficient listening skills we can never be sure that we have properly understood what we have been listening to. In speech things are said once only and if we miss them we have no opportunity to listen to them again. This is true of many lectures, meetings, speeches and broadcasts.

In lectures and many kinds of meetings, we have to be able to listen sufficiently well to be able to remember, and recall when necessary, important things that have been said. This kind of listening, as we shall see, is closely associated with the activity of notemaking.

At a time when so much is being communicated to us by means of the spoken word, we have to be able to discriminate and evaluate the relative significance and importance of a variety of utterances.

Critical listening is an essential component of efficient listening.

Seven Kinds of Listening

The listening activities we encounter fall into seven groups:

Simple listening

This category includes such everyday activities as telephone conversations, talking with friends and other conversational situations in which the listening is part of a more important social interaction rather than an activity in its own right. There is often little information of significance being communicated in such situations.

Discriminative listening

This term covers situations in which you are trying to separate sounds heard, so that not all the available sounds are listened to. Picking one sound out from others, for instance, trying to identify one bird singing among many or trying to listen to what one person is saying at a noisy party, could be described as discriminative listening.

Listening for relaxation

Here the activity is very close to mere hearing because the act of relaxing is what is important and the listening – to poetry, stories, recordings, broadcasts and the like – is secondary. You are listening in order to relax and have the mind and the attention diverted from everything else, rather than relaxing in order to listen.

Listening for information

This is one of the main forms of the active, purposeful, systematic listening referred to earlier and is the kind of activity required for assimilating announcements, listening to lectures, and so on. It is important here, as in the other kinds of listening which follow, to know as clearly as possible what it is that you require to know from the source being listened to.

Listening to organise ideas

In situations like lectures, discussions and meetings it is important to be able to discriminate between one person's voice and another's, and to listen effectively for information. In addition, it is essential to be able to organise your thoughts and ideas about the information and to sort out mentally the relationships between various pieces of information and ideas expressed. You must be able to assess the relative significance and importance of the various facts, ideas and opinions encountered, so that you emerge with a coherent and meaningful mental picture of what the lecture, discussion or meeting has been about. Unless you can organise both your own thoughts in this way and the expressed thoughts of others, you are at a serious disadvantage during many forms of social interaction.

Critical listening

In many ways, critical listening is similar to critical reading. Particular attention should be given, when listening critically, to both one's own purposes in listening (e.g. 'What do I need to know?') and to others' purposes in speaking (e.g. 'What are they trying to tell me?'). Attention should also be paid to the problems of identifying bias, emotion, exaggeration, propaganda and the like in what other people say. In these ways one is better equipped to reach an objective assessment.

Creative listening

In listening to music, drama, films and similar aesthetic experiences, there is more involvement than mere listening for pleasure or relaxation. The ability to discriminate between sound patterns is often required, as, for instance, in listening to music. The ability to assimilate the information contained in what is being listened to is important, as is the ability to organise the facts, ideas, themes and so on into meaningful wholes. Above all, for the greatest enjoyment and satisfaction to be obtained, the critical faculties should be active and the whole artistic creation appreciated in its total context. The more you know about a work, its creator, its predecessors, its philosophical or theoretical stimulus and its technique, the better your judgment and the more creatively fulfilling your listening will be.

People like students and managers will clearly be interested in the fourth, fifth and sixth kinds of listening described above. But if listening skills are to be fully developed, there must be practice in all kinds of listening, rather than a special concentration only on those which appear to be directly relevant to one's work or one's studies. In this way, breadth as well as depth is obtained and you are better able to develop a flexible, systematic approach to listening.

Listening is one of the laidback bear's favourite activities.

Methods of Improving Listening Skills

Seven methods of improving listening skills are outlined here. Together they provide a basis for a systematic, efficient and developmental approach to listening.

Notemaking

The efficient listener will always make notes where this can conveniently be done without inhibiting the person who is speaking. Memory is notoriously unreliable and, especially if reference may later have to be made to what has been said, a record of the content in note form can be invaluable.

> *Notes should be as concise as possible and should concentrate on the main points.*

Necessary details should be included within this framework. The aim should be to produce a short, coherent summary of the content of what has been said. The act of preparing these notes will help to improve the quality of the listening itself in many ways.

Defining purposes in listening

It is as important to know your purposes clearly when listening as it is in any other activity. Three factors will help you to define purposes.

1. **The nature of the material being listened to.** Form and content, length, relevance, etc.

2. **The reason for listening to it.** Why this particular material was selected, how much information is required from it, how the information will be used, etc.

3. **Expectations in listening.** What you expect to hear and how this satisfies reasons for listening, how useful the information is expected to be, how easy or difficult to understand, how interesting or dull, how entertaining or serious, etc.

After listening, the material should be reviewed and some assessment made of how far your purposes were satisfied and your expectations met. You should also consider how far defining purposes and expectations beforehand in this way improves the quality and efficiency of your listening.

Active involvement in listening

Because listening is a receptive activity, like reading, it is easy to allow it to become passive. This leads to a loss of listening ability, with consequent effects on the ability to base effective decisions on what has been listened to.

Active involvement is essential for efficient listening and most of the methods offered here for improving listening skills depend upon it for their success. Instead of simply sitting back and letting the information hit your eardrums, you should be actively listening for the information that will satisfy your purposes and expectations, as well as for information that is unexpected but relevant.

Attentiveness

This is the basis of active involvement and an effective counter to passivity. Your whole attention should, as far as possible, be given to whatever is being listened to. Only in this way can a proper assimilation and understanding of the information presented be obtained. Distractions should be avoided and notemaking will help to achieve this. 'Doodling' when making notes should be avoided, though it may be an indication that whatever is being listened to does not command the attention sufficiently and may not even be satisfying your purposes in listening enough to be worth continuing listening to.

Sensitivity

A perceptive listener must be sensitive to many aspects of the material he is listening to. It is not enough simply to be aware of the nature of the content, how it is organised and the purposes of the speaker as well as of the listener. There are a number of other factors you must also be sensitive to:

1. **Tone of voice.** This can totally alter the significance of a statement.

2. **Choice of words.** Many words have similar meanings, but the slight differences between them can be critical.

3. **Timing.** *When* something is said can be as important as *how* it is said.

4. **The speaker.** There are many ways in which a speaker's personality can affect what is said and its significance. One person says something and regardless of tone of voice, choice of words or something else, it is taken as a joke; another person says the same thing and offends people.

5. **The method of sound transmission.** In the case of broadcasts or recordings, the meaning and significance of something can be enhanced or impaired by the nature of the means to convey it. A speech will sound quite different when heard over a loudhailer outdoors from how it will sound on a good-quality tape recorder in a lounge.

6. **Your own role in encouraging easy, fluent interaction.** A listener can help a speaker immensely by showing an active interest in what is being said and by smiling, nodding and agreeing at the appropriate points.

Pattern of organisation

Except perhaps for long, rambling conversations of a personal, intimate nature, every discourse has a pattern of organisation. A speaker wants to say something and he organises it into an acceptable form before he begins to speak. If he does not, he may fail altogether to communicate with his listeners. In the case of broadcasts, pieces of music and other recordings, the presence of pattern will be even more evident. The efficient listener must be able to identify the pattern which has been imposed upon what he is listening to. It will often take the following form:

1. **Introduction.** The subject or theme is briefly stated or outlined.

2. **Development.** The subject or theme is explored, discussed or explained in greater detail along the lines indicated in the introduction.

3. **Conclusion.** The conclusions drawn in the development are restated for emphasis, or the audience is shown how the outline given in the introduction has been treated and given substance.

There are many variations which can be based on this simple pattern, but you should be able to identify these three basic elements in most of the material you encounter.

Critical listening

The advice given in Part 3, Chapter 22 on critical reading applies here as well and need not, therefore, be repeated. The main point which needs to be emphasised is that you should listen critically at all times.

Effective Speaking

Many people receive invitations to speak at meetings or conferences, or serve on committees or study groups. For those who are inexperienced in putting over a point of view, a methodical approach can save time and produce the confidence necessary for effective oral communication. One such approach is the **SPEAKER** method, which I have devised. It has six sections:

- ◆ **S**election of subject
- ◆ **P**reparation and Examination
- ◆ **A**udience assessment
- ◆ **K**eeping it brief
- ◆ **E**xpression
- ◆ **R**ehearsal

Selection of subject

If the choice is yours, select a theme which will enable you to convey some of your interest in it to your audience.

Preparation and Examination

You will speak more effectively if you are thoroughly familiar not only with the actual content of your speech but also with the topic in general. Examine your subject from all possible angles, so that you can approach it in a new way for your audience. Select no more than half a dozen main points to make.

Audience assessment

You should know:

- how many people you will be speaking to
- their approximate age range
- whether male or female or both
- whether the occasion will be formal or informal
- the kind of room or hall you will be speaking in
- any peculiar features about the audience.

Keeping it brief

This is perhaps the most important feature of the construction of any speech or lecture. The plan of your speech will be:

1. **Introduction.** Tell them what you will be talking about.
2. **Body of the speech.** Develop your points (no more than six).
3. **Conclusion.** A brief summary of the main points made.

Expression

Speak naturally and avoid both overformality and a too casual approach.

- Speak with the aid of notes but have a full transcript ready in case you 'dry up'.
- Number the sheets of your notes and the points you wish to make clearly, so that you do not confuse the order in which you want to say things.

◆ Speak distinctly so that people at the back can hear you, but do not shout.

◆ Avoid mannerisms and poses and too much walking about.

◆ Use concrete examples, illustrations and (if they come naturally to you) anecdotes to reinforce the points you are making.

Rehearsal

Whenever possible, practise your speech beforehand in private or in front of a sympathetic but critical friend. A tape recorder is useful here as it will tell you how you will sound to your audience.

Oral Reports, Presentations and Briefings

Basically, there is little difference between a written report and an oral report (or presentation or briefing). What differences there are lie in the delivery of the report, rather than in the stages that precede this. The work on which an oral report is based or the information collected may well be the same as that for a written report.

An oral report should be planned in a similar way to a written report, dividing itself into three basic sections:

1. Introduction.
2. Body of the report.
3. Conclusion.

To put it simply: in the **introduction** you will tell your audience what you are going to speak about or show them; in the **body of the report** you will tell them accurately and logically all that you want to say about the particular subject, and show them your charts, graphs and other aids; and in the **conclusion** you will summarise what you have said and shown, picking out the most important points for further emphasis and repetition.

The main differences between oral and written reports lie in the manner in which you speak. In a written report, slang and colloquial expressions are completely inappropriate, but this may not be the case with all oral reports.

You should talk to your audience in the manner which seems most natural and most likely to establish a favourable relationship between them and yourself.

If you don't establish this relationship, you will have the feeling that you have not secured the full attention of your audience, and this is bound to affect your ability to put across effectively what you have to say.

Oral reports or lectures should never be read. You should take notes on what you want to say, using similar headings to those you would use in a written report, and use them as a guide to what you want to tell your audience.

The purpose of notes lies in preventing you forgetting any important part of your report, rather than in providing you with the actual words to use.

No attempt should be made to memorise the report (this will make it sound unnatural, dull and uninteresting), although it does help if you can give a 'practice' talk beforehand when alone, or in the presence of a colleague who can be trusted to listen, criticise sympathetically and suggest improvements. This increases confidence.

Here are several further hints to successful public speaking:

1. If your mouth feels dry before you start, and there is no glass of water handy, relax your lower jaw, letting your lips scarcely touch each other, for a few moments. You will feel your mouth watering and the dryness will disappear. Alternatively, suck a fruit sweet or

chew some gum before going into the room or hall where the speech is to be made.

2. Remember the value of the pause in letting an important item of information sink in. Do not rush from statement to statement fearing that a pause means you have run dry. Never speak too quickly, and do not use long words if shorter ones will suit the purpose.

3. Use statistics carefully. Cut them down to a minimum as they rarely register when merely spoken. Put them in a handout or on a slide or overhead projector transparency and let them make a visual impact.

4. Avoid mannerisms and poses. Do not wander about restlessly, but move easily. Do not fiddle with your notes or other objects.

5. Treat your audience as human beings. Talk to them rather than at them and do not talk to the wall at the back of the room, or the window, ignoring your audience. Maintain 'eye contact' with members of the audience.

These points may help a little, but the main guides to follow in delivering an oral report, presentation or briefing (or speaking in public generally) are:

1. Know thoroughly what you are talking about.

2. Prepare your material carefully and speak with the aid of notes.

3. Practise what you are going to say at least once privately beforehand.

Chapter Twenty Five
SOCIAL SKILLS

The intention here is to expound briefly something of what is known about how and why people behave the way they do in social situations. This is done in the belief that this knowledge will help you to be more effective than a headless chicken in social interaction. And to be more like a persuasive laidback bear.

How People Interact with Each Other

Social behaviour is produced by at least seven types of drives or motivating forces:

1. **Biological drives which can produce social interaction.** For instance, the need for food and water.

2. **Dependency drives.** The need for the help, protection and guidance of others.

3. **Affiliation drives.** The need to be accepted and liked by others.

4. **Dominance drives.** The need to lead or control others.

5. **Sex drives.** The need for physical proximity, bodily contact and intimacy, usually with attractive members of the opposite sex.

6. **Aggression drives.** The desire to attack other people to accept your picture of yourself as valid.

7. **Self-esteem drives.** The need for other people to accept your picture of yourself as valid.

The motivation produced by these drives does not always operate the same way every time. For instance, biological needs seem to have equilibrium levels. Imbalances can be satisfied by obtaining, for example, food and water. This does not appear to apply to some other drives, like sex, where more can in fact increase your appetite.

Motivation can be conscious or unconscious. The effect of hypnotism is an example of the creation of unconscious motivation and there are other ways in which people can remain unaware of the reasons for a particular motivation to do something. One is the hidden influence of advertising in creating demand for various goods and services.

The degree of arousal and satisfaction of various drives can affect motivation and hence behaviour. There is usually an optimum level of arousal, which is lower with complex activities, and beyond which the effort to satisfy the drive becomes progressively less effective. Arousal is stronger when the incentive is larger, when the object of the motivation is wanted greatly and when its probability of being achieved is greater.

There are interrelationships between various social drives. Aggression, for example, is related to dominance and to low affiliation, but authoritarian personalities can be dominating or dependent on different occasions.

Communication With and Without Words

The social skills that people use include a wide range of levels of communication. These elements, which are combined into general patterns of behaviour, are as follows:

1. **Body contact.** For example, hand-shaking, patting on the back and caressing.

2. **Proximity and orientation.** For example, if one person is taller than another it puts him in a dominating position, and how close a person is allowed to approach will depend upon the degree of mutual acceptance.

3. **Gestures.** These help particularly to show emotional states.

4. **Facial expressions.** These too can indicate emotional states, and such things as perspiration can reveal nervous tension. Smiles are particularly important in getting along well with other people.

5. **Eye movements.** The kind of factors which are important here are where the eyes are looking and for how long, whether the gaze is furtive or open, and how much eye contact occurs between individuals – the greater this is, the greater the degree of intimacy.

6. **Non-verbal aspects of speech.** These include silences, errors, 'ers', tone of voice, loudness, pitch, speed of speaking, voice quality and smoothness.

7. **Speech.** We use speech to serve a wide range of purposes: asking questions, conveying information, giving instructions, influencing the behaviour of others by persuading, and so on.

When these elements are combined into general styles of behaviour, they produce examples like the following:

The affiliative style

The individual is warm and friendly. He allows other people to dominate. Since usually an intimate relationship develops only if those involved can interact more or less in the way they want, he tends to be successful socially. He avoids disagreements about beliefs, attitudes and almost anything else. He steers topics of conversation towards common bonds or interests. He treats others as equals and rewards them, for example, by taking an interest in them. His social interaction will contain high proportions of physical proximity, certain kinds of bodily contact (such as pats on the back), eye contact, smiling, friendly tones of voice and conversation about personal topics.

It is possible to establish a friendly relationship with almost any-body, but this entails further lines of action, such as not disagreeing, being more pleasant to them or being submissive, which may not always be palatable if you have to make friends with someone you dislike. It is also worth noting that, if techniques are overdone, the other person will 'run away'. It is essential to note the reactions of the other person and to react appropriately.

The dominant style

Dominant people tend to talk loud, fast and most of the time in a confident tone of voice. They interrupt others and control the topic of conversation. They need to combine sufficient warmth with these elements to avoid others withdrawing.

Generally speaking, dominant techniques only lead to a dominant relationship when combined with affiliative techniques, and the combination generates a more acceptable pattern of social behaviour.

It is possible to dominate, or influence another's behaviour, by the systematic rewarding of the desired behaviour immediately after it takes place, and the non-reward or punishment of other behaviour. Rewards based on the need for affiliation include smiling, eye contact, agreement, head-nodding, etc. Punishment might include frowning, looking away, looking bored, looking at a watch, disagreeing, etc. Other rewards and punishments can be based on needs for dominance, dependency, sex, or acceptance of the self-image. Another method of influence is to change the definition of the situation, suggesting that it is not what the other thought it was (for example, indicating that it is a party so they should be cheerful, or it is a serious meeting so they should stop being funny, or there are strangers present so they should be more discreet).

Other minor social styles

These involve, for example, 'presence' as opposed to 'informality' and the ability to establish 'rapport'.

Motivation is the main factor in the choice of social skills and styles. It is known that extroverts have stronger affiliative needs than others. Among the other things that we know about how people use their social skills is the fact that women engage in more eye contact and are more dependent on vision in social encounters than men.

What Happens When People Meet

The ways in which we normally categorise people – sex, age, social class, 'warmth' or 'coldness', introverts or extroverts, variations in anxiety or neuroticism, attitudes to authority – all determine the selection of social skills in dealing with different kinds of people. Introverts, for instance, respond better to praise and extroverts to blame.

When two people meet, the length and frequency of their meetings will generally depend on the rewards each receives from the other. They may have to balance their social skills and this may mean departing somewhat from their preferred techniques. For smooth interaction, synchronisation is necessary in:

1. the amount of speech each allows the other;
2. the speed or tempo of interaction;
3. who is allowed to dominate;
4. the degree of intimacy between them;
5. the amount of co-operation and competition;
6. the emotional tone of the interaction;
7. the task and procedure (for example, resolving problems of wanting to do different things or do the same thing in different ways).

When two people meet who are never likely to meet again, there is also a 'stranger value' which may increase the amount and speed of self-disclosure. This applies particularly when on holiday or in interviews. Normally, it takes longer periods of interaction to produce greater self-disclosure. Even the superficial details are disclosed most easily, though if two people are isolated intimate disclosure is increased, as it is if the disclosures are mutual.

Before meeting someone, what you are told about a person conditions your attitude and behaviour towards them. If you are told a person is friendly, then you will act in a friendly way and will evoke the same response in the other.

Quarrels are often the result of failures to synchronise in an increasingly intimate situation. The most important factors in friendship, for instance, are as follows:

1. People must meet, and in many cases the more frequently they do, the more they will tend to like each other.

2. Each person must significantly satisfy the needs of the other.

3. People with similar values and interests will tend to like each other. The intense conformity among groups of teenagers and students may explain why friendships made then are so long-lasting.

4. People with similar personality traits will tend to like each other.

5. Opposites can attract each other when, for instance, one is dominant and the other submissive.

6. A similar process can occur when one confirms the other's role (for example, pupil and teacher).

7. One person will tend to like another if he sees that the other likes him.

8. One person may like another if he sees he can be helpful or useful to him and may even establish a 'reciprocity' each doing things for the other.

There is a small statistical tendency for people high in the following traits to be more popular than those who are low:

1. **Extraversion.** Having a lively and outgoing personality.

2. **Emotional adjustment.** Being emotionally stable and not moody.

3. **Social sensitivity.** Expressed in such things as consideration for others and being able to see things from other people's points of view.

4. **Intelligence**.

But more important are the following:

1. **The extent to which a person conforms to group norms** (i.e., behaves as other members of the group behave).

2. **The extent to which a person manifests the ideals of the group** (i.e., has the same aims and principles as other members of the group).

3. **The extent to which a person contributes to the group's activities.**

This explains why a person can be highly popular in one group or social setting, but completely rejected in another.

How groups behave

Dyads (groups of two people) are less stable than larger groups. There is more danger of the interaction collapsing and there are more signs of tension. However, there is usually less expression of agreement and disagreement.

Triads (groups of three people) show various kinds of internal competition and jockeying for position. If there are three men, there is likely to be a straight battle for dominance. If there are two males and one female, the males will normally compete for the attention of the female. If, however, there are three females, and one is left out, the others will generally work to keep her in. If there is one powerful and dominating member of a triad, the others may form a coalition and combine against him.

As group size increases from four to ten

◆ it becomes less easy to participate and influence what the others will do

◆ there is a greater discrepancy between the amount of interaction of different members (in large groups the majority may scarcely speak at all)

- there are greater differences in styles of behaviour
- there is often more expression of disagreement
- there is usually more division of labour if there is work to do.

Most people prefer to belong to a group of five or six, since this gives them variety while they can still exert influence over the others.

Groups develop definite 'pecking orders' in terms of the amount of speech and influence permitted to each member. Techniques of reward and punishment, of the kind discussed earlier, can be used to maintain the hierarchy. Norms of behaviour are developed and there are pressures to conform, with rejection if any individual fails to. A deviate (one who refuses to conform to group norms) becomes the object of considerable attention and of efforts to persuade him to change his behaviour. There is an exception for people of very high informal status by virtue of their contribution to the group. They earn 'idiosyncrasy credit', or permission to deviate. An example would be the 'clown' who does outrageous things, but in such a way as to make people laugh.

The nature of the task the group has to face is a major factor in determining the status hierarchy and general behaviour. If group members are to share equally in the group product, they will tend to cooperate; if the best performer is to take all, they will tend to compete.

Under a cooperative motivation, group members help each other more, there is more division of labour and they come to like one another. Under competition, hostile attitudes often develop.

Headless chickens become very agitated under conditions of competition. Laidback bears take things in their stride. They know that cooperation leads to a much more relaxed and productive approach, and this is the ultimate goal of all laidback bears.

INDEX

If you want to know how...

- ◆ To buy a home in the sun, and let it out
- ◆ To move overseas, and work well with the people who live there
- ◆ To get the job you want, in the career you like
- ◆ To plan a wedding, and make the Best Man`s speech
- ◆ To build your own home, or manage a conversion
- ◆ To buy and sell houses, and make money from doing so
- ◆ To gain new skills and learning, at a later time in life
- ◆ To empower yourself, and improve your lifestyle
- ◆ To start your own business, and run it profitably
- ◆ To prepare for your retirement, and generate a pension
- ◆ To improve your English, or write a PhD
- ◆ To be a more effective manager, and a good communicator
- ◆ To write a book, and get it published

If you want to know how to do all these things and much, much more...

howto books

If you want to know how ...
to be an effective mentor

"Mentoring is an exclusive one-to-one relationship, is completely confidential and can be a useful complement to other staff development tools. This book explains what mentoring is ... and what it is not! It takes you stage by stage through the process and shows how it can be of benefit to and an opportunity for development, both for the person being mentored and for the mentor."

David Kay and Roger Hinds

A Practical Guide to Mentoring

David Kay and Roger Hinds

"This book works through the process easily with simple steps and practical guidance, aided by an easy-to-follow contents section ... A handy and quick reference text for mentors." Training Journal

ISBN 1 85703 812 6

If you want to know how ... to resolve conflict in the workplace

Margaret and Shay McConnon show you how to manage disagreements and develop trust and understanding. They enable us to begin meeting our needs and those of the other person, while maintaining the relationship and resolving our differences respectfully.

Resolving Conflict

Shay and Margaret McConnon

'One of the best books I have read on conflict resolution in my 30+ years in the field.' Mediation Office The World Bank

If you want to know how ...
to read faster and recall more

In today's information laden world, time is valuable. Reports, reference books, contracts, correspondence, newspapers, magazines and journals are just some of the things you might need to read and digest on a daily basis.

If you feel that the speed at which you read these items and the extent to which you are able to retain their information could be improved, then the use of the practical tips, proven techniques and numerous practise exercises in this book could help you to reach your potential. With the aid of this invaluable book, you can save time and achieve more.

Read Faster, Recall More

Use proven techniques for speed reading and maximum recall
Gordon Wainwright

"...will help you to reduce the time spent on reading and recalling information." – Evening Standard

"...purely practical and aims to help you in the professional environment." – The Times

"A worthwhile investment." – The Guardian

ISBN 1 85703 936 X

If you want to know how ... to make meetings work effectively

Handled well, meetings can be invaluable tools for getting things discussed, agreed and then taken forward. Whether you're chairing or attending, this book will enable you to have meetings that are productive and get things done.

Make Meetings Work

JULIE-ANN AMOS

'This is a great book ... a short guide to making meetings work. There are excellent sections on agenda setting, managing the meeting, communicating and concluding.' Training Jourmal

ISBN 1 85703 816 9

How To Books are available through all good bookshops, or you can order direct from us through Grantham Book Services.

Tel: +44 (0)1476 541080
Fax: +44 (0)1476 541061
Email: orders@gbs.tbs-ltd.co.uk

Or via our website:

www.howtobooks.co.uk

To order via any of these methods please quote the title(s) of the book(s) and your credit card number together with its expiry date.

For further information about our books and catalogue, please contact:

How To Books
3 Newtec Place
Magdalen Road
Oxford OX4 1RE

Visit our web site at

www.howtobooks.co.uk

Or you can contact us by email at info@howtobooks.co.uk